DA LOVE-ANANDA GITA
(THE FREE GIFT OF THE DIVINE LOVE-BLISS)

The Five Books Of
The Heart Of The Adidam Revelation

BOOK THREE

The "Late-Time" Avataric Revelation
Of The Great Means To Worship and To Realize
The True and Spiritual Divine Person
(The egoless Personal Presence Of Reality and Truth,
Which <u>Is</u> The Only <u>Real</u> God)

By
The Divine World-Teacher,
RUCHIRA AVATAR
ADI DA SAMRAJ

THE DAWN HORSE
MIDDLETOWN,

D1477643

NOTE TO THE READER

All who study Adidam (the Way of the Heart) or take up its practice should remember that they are responding to a Call to become responsible for themselves. They should understand that they, not Avatar Adi Da Samraj or others, are responsible for any decision they may make or action they take in the course of their lives of study or practice.

The devotional, Spiritual, functional, practical, relational, cultural, and formal community practices and disciplines referred to in this book are appropriate and natural practices that are voluntarily and progressively adopted by each student-novice and member of Adidam and adapted to his or her personal circumstance. Although anyone may find them useful and beneficial, they are not presented as advice or recommendations to the general reader or to anyone who is not a student-novice or a member of Adidam. And nothing in this book is intended as a diagnosis, prescription, or recommended treatment or cure for any specific "problem", whether medical, emotional, psychological, social, or Spiritual. One should apply a particular program of treatment, prevention, cure, or general health only in consultation with a licensed physician or other qualified professional.

Da Love-Ananda Gita (The Free Gift Of The Divine Love-Bliss) is formally authorized for publication by the Ruchira Sannyasin Order of the Tantric Renunciates of Adidam, as part of the Standard Edition of the Divine "Source-Texts" of the Divine World-Teacher, Ruchira Avatar Adi Da Samraj. (The Ruchira Sannyasin Order of the Tantric Renunciates of Adidam is the senior Spiritual and Cultural Authority within the formal gathering of formally acknowledged devotees of the Divine World-Teacher, Ruchira Avatar Adi Da Samraj.)

NOTE TO BIBLIOGRAPHERS: The correct form for citing Ruchira Avatar Adi Da Samraj's Name (in any form of alphabetized listing) is:

Adi Da Samraj, Ruchira Avatar

Previously published as
The Love-Ananda Gita and
The Santosha Avatara Gita
First edition, July 1989
Standard edition, enlarged and updated, September 1990
Standard edition, updated, July 1995
Standard edition, enlarged and updated, April 1998
Printed in the United States of America

Produced by the Eleutherian Pan-Communion of Adidam
in cooperation with the Dawn Horse Press

International Standard Book Number: 1-57097-051-3
Library of Congress Catalog Card Number: 98-71203

CONTENTS

DA LOVE-ANANDA GITA
(THE FREE GIFT OF THE DIVINE LOVE-BLISS
39

FIRST WORD
Do Not Misunderstand <u>Me</u>—
I Am <u>Not</u> "Within" <u>you</u>, but you <u>Are</u> In <u>Me</u>, and
I Am <u>Not</u> a Mere "Man" in the "Middle" of Mankind,
but All of Mankind Is Surrounded,
and Pervaded, and Blessed By <u>Me</u>
41

Ruchira Avatar Adi Da Samraj
Adidam Samrajashram (Naitauba), Fiji, 1997

The All-Surpassing Revelation of The Divine World-Teacher, Ruchira Avatar Adi Da Samraj

by
Carolyn Lee, Ph.D.

The *Da Love-Ananda Gita* communicates a Revelation of the Divine surpassing anything that has ever been known in the conditionally manifested worlds. The Appearance here, in human Form, of the Supreme Giver, Ruchira Avatar Adi Da Samraj, is that Revelation, the Revelation of God Incarnate—Come to Bless and Awaken all beings in all realms to the All-Surpassing Truth and "Brightness"[1] of the Divine Reality. Ruchira Avatar Adi Da is the Promised God-Man. His Coming is the Love-Response of the Divine, in Person, to eons of prayer and longing, on the part of beings everywhere, to be restored to the Heart of Real God.[2]

The Appearance of the Ruchira Avatar, Adi Da Samraj, truly is <u>the</u> Great Event of history. It is the Event that Reveals the real meaning of the entire past, and the Great Purpose of all future time. His Avataric Incarnation[3] is the fruition of an infinitely vast Divine Process, originating before time and space itself, and developing throughout the Cosmic domain in response to the desperate prayers

---

Carolyn Lee is a formal renunciate practitioner of the Way of Adidam living at Adidam Samrajashram (Fiji), the Great Island-Hermitage of the Ruchira Avatar, Adi Da Samraj.

Notes for this Introduction can be found on pp. 25-28.

of beings everywhere, suffering the pain of apparent separation from Real God. In that unspeakable sweep of time, there have been unique beings who, through great struggle and sacrifice, made "windows" to the Divine for others. They gave Teachings and practices, were worshipped and honored, and have become the source of the entire human tradition of religion and Spirituality. Again and again, it has seemed to those alive in a particular time and place that the revelation was complete, the salvation perfect, the enlightenment given.

Even so, there has remained a thread of prophecy in all the great Spiritual traditions foretelling One yet to Appear, One Who must Come in the darkest time of humanity, when the world is at its worst, and bring to completion all the revelations of the past. Christians await the second coming of Jesus; Muslims, the Mahdhi (the last prophet); Buddhists, Maitreya (the coming Buddha); and Hindus, the Kalki Avatar (the final Avatar of Vishnu). Even as recently as February 1939, a celebrated Indian Adept, Upasani Baba, prophesied the imminent appearance of a Western-born Avatar, who "will be all-powerful and bear down everything before Him."[4]

True to the ancient intuitions about the Promised God-Man, Avatar Adi Da Samraj Appears now in this "dark" epoch of the decay of the great religious and Spiritual traditions, East and West. He Appears in an era when our very survival is threatened, not only by sophisticated weapons of war, but also by the destruction of human culture—and even of our total environment—through the heartless machine of scientific and political materialism. Avatar Adi Da Samraj has Come, miraculously, in an extreme time, when His "radical"[5] Truth and His Divine Grace are most sorely needed, to allay the forces of destruction. As He has Said Himself, it may take thousands of years for the significance of His Birth—the Descent of the Divine Person into cosmic space and time—to be fully appreciated. But His Revelation has now perfectly and irrevocably occurred.

After more than a quarter of a century of living in His Company, participating in His direct face-to-face Teaching Work with thousands of people, feeling the indescribable Transmission of Spirit-Force that Radiates from Him, and witnessing the limitless scope of His Divine Power to transform beings and conditions near and far, we, the devotees of Avatar Adi Da, freely profess our recognition that He is that All-Completing God-Man promised for the "dark" epoch—He is "the 'late-time' Avataric Revelation" of the Divine Person. Reading this book will enable you to make this supreme discovery for yourself.

The Divine Names of the Ruchira Avatar

There are several parts to the Divine Title and Name of Ruchira Avatar Adi Da Samraj, each of which expresses an aspect of our recognition of Him. "Ruchira" (meaning "Radiant", "Effulgent", or "Bright") is the Condition of All-Pervading Radiance, Joy, and Love-Blissful Divine Consciousness, Which He, even in His infancy, named "the 'Bright'". Avatar Adi Da Samraj Is the unique Revelation of the "Bright"—and, because this is so, He is the Ruchira "Avatar", or the "Shining Divine 'Descent'", the Appearance of Real God in bodily (human) Form.

"Adi Da", the Principal Name of our Beloved Guru, is a sublime Mystery in itself. In 1979, He Assumed the Divine Name "Da", an ancient reference for Real God (first spontaneously Revealed to Him in 1970), a Name that means "the Giver". In 1994, the Name "Adi" (meaning "First", or "Source") came to Him spontaneously as the complement to His Principal Name, "Da". Thus, to call upon the Ruchira Avatar via the Name "Adi Da" is to Invoke Him as the Divine Giver and Source-Person, the Primordial and Eternal Being of Grace.

Avatar Adi Da is also "Samraj", the "Universal Ruler", or "Supreme Lord"—not in any worldly or political sense,

11

but as the Divine Master of all hearts and the Spiritual King of all who resort to Him. Thus, when we approach Avatar Adi Da Samraj, we are not at all approaching an ordinary man, or even a remarkable saint or yogi or sage. We are approaching Real God in Person.

The Divine Body of Real God

The All-Surpassing God-Man, Adi Da Samraj, is Imbued with extraordinary Siddhis, or Divine Powers, that allow Him to Bless and Liberate beings on the scale of Totality. While He may appear, on the ordinary level, to be Working with particular human beings in His immediate Company, He is, at the same time, Doing His Miraculous Work with events and conditions in the natural world, in the human world, and in the domain of non-human beings, and even in all realms.

Thus, the Ruchira Avatar is simultaneously Present in every gross and subtle plane of the cosmos. His bodily human Form, therefore, is just the minutest part of the Grand Scale of His Being, the part that has "Emerged" into visibility. His visible bodily (human) Form in this world, or His Form in any other world, is a Link, a Sign, a Means by Which beings may Find Him As He Is altogether, Spiritually Pervading everything and, at the same time, Standing Prior to all that exists—As Consciousness Itself, or Inherently Love-Blissful, Self-Radiant Being Itself.

The bodily (human) Form of Adi Da Samraj is the touch-point, the Agency, by Which He is making Himself known in this world. He is Revealing that the Divine is not an abstraction, an idea, an essence, something to philosophize about. The Divine Is here in Person.

There is a long tradition of describing the Divine in personal terms—as, for example, the "Creator-God" (or "Father" figure) of popular religion. But the Revelation of Ruchira Avatar Adi Da Samraj shows that many such popular concepts of the Divine do not have anything to do with Real God. The God-Man of Infinite "Brightness" Reveals Himself as the One and <u>Only</u> Person, the Divine Heart of all that <u>is</u>, and, ultimately, the only True Identity of every one and every thing.

The experience of beholding our Beloved Guru goes far beyond the mere perceiving of His human physical Body. He is the Person of Real God, known <u>most</u> intimately and ecstatically through the Revelation of His Divine Body—the Infinitely Expansive, Radiantly "Bright" Form of Real God:

AVATAR ADI DA SAMRAJ: My Divine Form Is the "Bright", the Love-Bliss-Form That you can feel tangibly Touching you, Surrounding you, Moving in you, Making all kinds of changes. That Is My Divine Body. I can Manifest It anywhere, and Do, all the time. I Manifest My Self.

My Divine Body will Exist Forever. Therefore, My devotees will be able to experience Me directly, Bodily—My "Bright" Body, My Very Person—Forever. [August 11, 1995]

Through His unparalleled Teaching Word, through the miraculous stories of His Divine Play with people everywhere, and, sooner or later, through the Touch of His Divine Body, Avatar Adi Da converts your heart to Real God—to <u>Him</u>—and "Brightens" your entire body-mind.

The Three Great Purposes
of the Ruchira Avatar

From the moment of His Birth (in New York, November 3, 1939), the Divine Incarnation of Grace, Adi Da Samraj, was Consciously Aware of the "Bright" as His Native Divine Condition. But then, at the age of two years, Avatar Adi Da made a profound but spontaneous choice. He chose to relinquish His constant Enjoyment of the "Bright" out of what He Describes as a "painful loving", a sympathy for the suffering and ignorance of human beings. Our Beloved Guru Confesses that He chose to "Learn Man", to enter into everything that mankind feels and suffers, in order to discover how to Draw mankind into His own "Bright" Divine Condition.

This utterly remarkable Submission to the ordinary human state was the first Purpose of the Avataric Incarnation of Adi Da Samraj. In His Spiritual autobiography, *The Knee Of Listening*, Avatar Adi Da recounts this amazing and "Heroic" Ordeal, which lasted for the first thirty years of His Life. It was not until 1970 that He Re-Awakened Most Perfectly[6] and Permanently to the "Bright", and embarked upon the second great Purpose of His Incarnation, the Process of <u>Teaching</u> Man.

The Teaching Work of our Beloved Guru was completely unique. He did not give formal public discourses, nor was He ever, in any sense, a public teacher. He simply made Himself available to all who were willing to enter into the living Process of Real God-Realization in His Company, a Process Which He summarized as the <u>relationship</u> to Him. Through that relationship—a most extraordinary human and Spiritual intimacy—Avatar Adi Da Samraj perfectly Embraced each of His devotees,

using every kind of Skillful Means to Awaken them to the Truth that the separate, un-Enlightened self—with all its fear, anxieties, and fruitless <u>seeking</u> for Happiness—is only an illusion. Happiness, He Revealed, Is

Always <u>Already</u> the Case and may be <u>Realized</u> in every moment of heart-Communion with Him.

In 1986, an Event occurred that brought to culmination the Great Love-Sacrifice of the Ruchira Avatar. In this Great Event, a profound Yogic Swoon overwhelmed His body-mind, and Avatar Adi Da Samraj relinquished His entire Ordeal of Learning and Teaching Man. In the wake of that great Swoon, He simply Radiated His Divinity as never before. He had "Emerged" in the Fullness of His Being, the Form of Real God Pouring forth His Love-Blessing to all universally. This was the beginning of His eternally proceeding Divine "Emergence". From that moment, the Divine Lord, Adi Da, has devoted Himself to the third and eternal Purpose of His Avataric Incarnation—that of Blessing Man (and even all beings). He is now Merely Present, Radiating His Heart-Blessing, Transmitting the Love-Bliss Force of the Divine Person to all the billions of human beings in this world and to the numberless beings on all planes crying out for Real God.

The End of the Twenty-Five Year Revelation

Even after the Great Event in 1986 that initiated His Divine "Emergence", the All-Completing God-Man continued to Work to ensure that His Revelation of the Way of Adidam, the unique Divine Way of Realizing Real God, was fully and firmly founded in the world. It was not until March 1997, at the time of writing *Hridaya Rosary* (on the Spiritual Process of Communion with Him in His "Bright" Divine Body) that Avatar Adi Da Samraj Declared that all the foundation Work of His Incarnation had been completely and finally Done.

The inexpressible Divine Sacrifice of Avatar Adi Da Samraj is Full. Everything, absolutely everything, for the total understanding and right practice of the real religious process culminating in Divine Enlightenment has been Said and Done by Him. The summary of His Divine Wisdom-Teaching—Written and Perfected by Him in vast detail—is preserved for all time in His twenty-three "Source-Texts". And His Divine Way, the Way of Adidam, is fully established. All in all, this monumental Work has taken Avatar Adi Da a quarter of a century—twenty-five years of unrelenting Struggle to make His Avataric Incarnation real in the hearts and body-minds of His devotees.

Now, in the epoch of His World-Blessing Work, Avatar Adi Da simply remains at His Great Island-Hermitage, Adidam Samrajashram, in Fiji, except when He is moved to travel for the sake of His Blessing of all. He lives as the Supreme "Ruchira Tantric Sannyasin",[7] the Free Renunciate Who has Transcended everything and Who is, therefore, Free to Embrace everything—all beings, forms, worlds, and all experience—for the sake of Drawing all into the Most Perfect Realization of Real God.

The "Bright" Divine Guru, Adi Da, is not an ordinary man. Neither is He merely an extraordinary man. He is not a social personality. He is not bound by ordinary conventions and rules of behavior. He is not a "figure-head" Guru, who simply presides at ceremonial occasions. No, Avatar Adi Da Samraj is the Divine <u>Avadhoot</u>,[8] the truly Free One, Who Knows what is really necessary to Liberate beings.

The True Avadhoot Speaks and Acts the Truth without restraint. He does not smile at the ego's posturing and foolishness. Avatar Adi Da Samraj <u>is</u> a Fire, a Fire of Love-Bliss, Who Consumes and Transforms and "Brightens" all who approach Him for the authentic Process of Divine Enlightenment. He has Come to bring an end to the reign of "Narcissus", the hard-hearted and Godless ego-"I".

16

The Way of Adidam

The immense struggle and Sacrifice that Beloved Adi Da had to endure in order to make His Revelation of the Divine Way of Adidam was the result of the enormous difficulty that human beings—especially in this ego-glorifying "late-time"—have with the Process of truly ego-transcending religion. People prefer not to confront the real Process of ego-transcendence. They prefer forms of religion based on a system of beliefs and a code of moral and social behavior. But this kind of ordinary religion, as Avatar Adi Da has always pointed out, does not go to the core, to the root-suffering of human beings. This is because ordinary religion, rather than going beyond the ego-principle, is actually based on it: the ego-self stands at the center, and the Divine is sought and appealed to as the great Power that is going to save and satisfy the individual self. Avatar Adi Da Describes such religion as "client-centered".

In contrast to conventional religion, there is the Process that Avatar Adi Da calls true religion, religion that is centered in the Divine in response to a true Spiritual Master, who has, to at least some significant degree, Realized Real God (as opposed to merely offering teachings about God). Thus, true religion does not revolve around the individual's desires for any kind of "spiritual" consolations or experience—it is self-transcending, rather than self-serving. True religion based on self-surrendering Guru-devotion certainly has existed for thousands of years, but the ecstatic news of this book is that now the Divine Person, Real God, is directly Present, Functioning as Guru, Alive in bodily (human) Form to receive the surrender and the worship of those who recognize and respond to Him. Therefore, the Ruchira-Guru, Adi Da, is the Way of Adidam.

AVATAR ADI DA SAMRAJ: The Way of Adidam is the Way That is <u>always</u> Prior to and Beyond all seeking. In order for the Way of Adidam to be Generated, it was necessary for Me to be Incarnated, and Transmitted in place, in this place, in the extremity—in the place where the Divine is otherwise not proposed, or only sought. This was necessary, in order to Demonstrate that I Am That One Who Is Always Already The Case, and in order to Communicate the Way of non-seeking, or the Way of transcending egoity in <u>this</u> circumstance of arising (or in any circumstance of arising).

The "problem" is not that the Divine is "Elsewhere". The "problem" is that <u>you</u> are the <u>self-contraction</u>. This understanding, Given by My Grace, makes it possible to Realize the Divine Self-Condition Most Perfectly, <u>As Is</u>, no matter what is arising. But Such Most Perfect Realization is not merely Realization of the Divine as an abstract (or merely philosophically proposed) "Reality". Most Perfect Realization (or Most Perfect "Knowledge") of the Divine is the Divine "Known" by Means of My Revelation, "Known" <u>As</u> My Revelation.

<u>I</u> Came to <u>you</u>. Therefore, the Way of Adidam is based on your <u>receiving</u> Me, not on your <u>seeking</u> for Me.

Thus, That Which is proposed by seekers as the <u>goal</u> (or the achievement at the end) is the <u>beginning</u> (or the very Gift) of the Way for My devotees. ["I <u>Am</u> The Avatar Of One", from Part Two of *He-<u>and</u>-She Is <u>Me</u>*]

The word "Adidam" is derived from the Name of Ruchira Avatar Adi Da, because it is the religion founded on devotional recognition of Him and Spiritual resort to Him. This Spiritual resort to Adi Da Samraj is a moment to moment practice of surrendering every aspect of the being—mind, emotion, breath, and body—to Him. Such whole-bodily surrender to the Living One opens the heart to Joy. Thus, there is no <u>struggle</u> to overcome egoity or to achieve Oneness with Adi Da Samraj. The Happiness of heart-Communion with Him is available in every moment. In His Spiritual Company, therefore, there is not anything to seek. All the traditional goals of religion—the search for the Vision of God, or for Oneness with Reality via the samadhis, satoris, and mystical experiences described in the traditions—all of this falls away when the heart falls in love with Adi Da Samraj. He is Perfect Satisfaction, because He is Real God, the Very Source and Giver of true religion. The Realization, or Enlightenment, that He Offers in the Way of Adidam is Divine Self-Realization, Divine Enlightenment, Prior to all experience high or low. "Mankind", as Avatar Adi Da Says, "does not know the Way to the Divine Domain"—the ego does not know. Only the Divine Person Knows. Only the Divine Person, Incarnate as Guru, can Show you the Way to the Divine Domain.

Avatar Adi Da Samraj is directly Generating the Divine Process of Most Perfect Liberation in all His devotees who have vowed to embrace the total practice of the Way of Adidam.[9] The Process unfolds by His Grace, according to the depth of surrender and response in His devotee. The most extraordinary living testimonies to the Greatness and Truth of the Way of Adidam are Ruchira Adidama Sukha Dham Naitauba and Ruchira Adidama Jangama Hriddaya Naitauba, the two members of the Adidama Quandra Mandala of the Ruchira Avatar.[10] These remarkable women devotees have totally consecrated themselves to Avatar Adi Da, and live always in His Sphere, in a relationship of unique intimacy and service. By their profound love of, and most exemplary surrender to, their Divine Heart-Master, they have become combined with Him at a unique depth. They manifest the Yogic signs of deep and constant Immersion in His Divine Being, both in meditation and daily life. Ruchira Adidama Sukha Dham and Ruchira Adidama Jangama Hriddaya are also members of the Ruchira Sannyasin Order of the Tantric Renunciates of Adidam (the senior cultural authority within the formal gathering of Avatar Adi Da's devotees), practicing in the context of the

**Avatar Adi Da Samraj with Ruchira Adidama Sukha Dham (left)
and Ruchira Adidama Jangama Hriddaya (right)**

ultimate stages (or the "Perfect Practice") of the total Way of Adidam.

After more than twenty years of intense testing by their Beloved Guru, the Adidama Quandra Mandala have demonstrated themselves to be singular devotees, the first representatives of humankind to truly recognize Him As He <u>Is</u>. Through their profound recognition of Him, Avatar Adi Da has been able to lead the Adidama Quandra Mandala to the threshold of Divine Enlightenment. And, even now, day by day, He continues to Work with them to make their Realization of Him Most Perfect. The profound and ecstatic relationship that the Adidama Quandra Mandala live with Avatar Adi Da hour to hour can be felt in this letter of devotional confession to Him by Ruchira Adidama Sukha Dham:

RUCHIRA ADIDAMA SUKHA DHAM: Bhagavan Love-Ananda,[11] Supreme and Divine Person, Real-God-Body of Love, I rest in Your Constant and Perfect Love-Embrace with no need but to forever worship you. Suddenly in love, Mastered at heart, always with my head at Your Supreme and Holy Feet, I am beholding and recognizing

Your Divine Body and "Bright" Divine Person. My Beloved, You so "Brightly" Descend and utterly Convert this heart, mind, body, and breath, from separate self to the "Bhava"[12] of Your Love-Bliss-Happiness.

Supreme Lord Ruchira, in the profound depths of Ruchira Sannyas (since my Initiation into formal Ruchira Sannyas on December 18, 1994), the abandonment of the former personality, the relinquishment of ego-bondage to the world, and the profound purification and release brought about by my now almost twenty-four years of love and worship of You has culminated in a great comprehensive force in my one-pointed devotion to You and a great certainty in the Inherent Sufficiency of Realization Itself. The essence, or depth, of my practice is to always remain freely submitted and centralized in You, the Feeling of Being, the Condition Prior to all bondage, all modification, and all illusion.

My Beloved Lord Ruchira, You have Moved this heart-feeling and awareness to renounce all "bonding" with conditionally manifested others, conditionally manifested worlds, and conditionally manifested self, to enter into the depths of this "in-love" and utter devotion to You. I renounce all in order to Realize You and to exist eternally in Your House. Finding You has led to the revelation of a deep urge to abandon all superficiality and to simply luxuriate in Your Divine Body and Person. All separation is shattered in Your Divine Love-Bliss-"Bhava". Your Divine and Supreme Body Surrounds and Pervades all. Your Infusion is Utter. I feel You everywhere.

I am Drawn by Grace of Your Spiritual (and Always Blessing) Presence into profound meditative Contemplation of Your Very (and Inherently Perfect) State. Sometimes, when I am entering into these deep states of meditation, I remain vaguely aware of the body, and particularly of the breath and the heartbeat. I feel the heart and lungs slow down and become very loud-sounding. Then I am sometimes aware of my breath and heartbeat ceasing temporarily, or being suspended in a state of Yogic sublimity, and I quickly lose bodily consciousness. Then there is no body, no mind, no perceptual awareness, and no conceptual awareness. There is only abiding in Contemplation of You in Your Domain of Consciousness Itself. I feel You literally <u>Are</u> me, and, when I resume association with the body and begin once again to hear my breath and heartbeat, I feel the remarkable Power of Your Great Samadhi. I feel no necessity for anything, and I feel Your Capability to Bless and Change and Meditate all, in Your Place. I can feel how this entrance into objectless worship of You As Consciousness Itself (allowing this Abiding to deepen ever so profoundly, by utter submission of separate self to You) establishes me in a different relationship to everything that arises.

My Beloved Bhagavan, Love-Ananda, I have Found You. Now I can behold You and live in this constant Embrace. This is my Joy and Happiness and the Yoga of ego-renunciation I engage. [October 11, 1997]

Inherent in this profound confession is the certainty that there is no lasting happiness to be found in this world or in any world. The only real Happiness, the Happiness that infinitely exceeds all human dreams of Happiness, is the All-Outshining Bliss and Love of Heart-Identification with the Supreme Giver, Adi Da Samraj.

AVATAR ADI DA SAMRAJ: Absolutely NOTHING conditional is satisfactory. Everything conditional disappears—everything. This fact should move the heart to cling to Me, to resort to Me, to take refuge in Me. This is why people become devotees of Mine. This is the reason for the religious life. The unsatisfactoriness of conditional existence requires resort to the Divine Source, and the Realization of the Divine Source-Condition. [August 9, 1997]

The Supreme Grace of a Human Life

Avatar Adi Da knew from His childhood that He had Come to "save the world". He even confessed as much to a relative who questioned him one day about what He wanted to do when He grew up.[13] But He did not mean this in any conventionally religious, or politically idealistic, sense. He has never taught a consoling belief system that promises "heaven" after death or a utopian existence on this earth. No, He has Come to set in motion a universal heart-conversion, a conversion from the self-destructive and other-destructive ego-life of separativeness to a life of "unqualified relatedness", or boundless all-embracing love.

Never before in the history of mankind has there been a moment like this one. You do not have to suffer the fear of death and all the dead-ends of ordinary life for one more day, because the Ultimate Mystery has been Unveiled, the Very Truth of Existence has been Revealed. You have the opportunity to enter into relationship with the One Who <u>Is</u> Reality Itself, Truth Itself, and the Only

Real God. That One, Adi Da Samraj, is humanly Alive now, and, even in this moment, is Blessing all with Inexpressible Grace, Perfect Mastery, and Unlimited Power.

What else could be truly satisfying? What else deserves the sacrifice of your egoity and the love-surrender of your entire body-mind?

Nothing can match the Great Process of Adidam that Avatar Adi Da is Offering you. When you become His formal devotee and take up the Way of Adidam, He leads you beyond the dreadful illusions of separateness and alienation. He Instructs you in the right form of every detail of your existence. He Converts the motion of your life from anxious seeking and egoic self-concern to the Bliss of self-forgetting Love-Communion with Him.

Avatar Adi Da Samraj is here only to Love you. He Lives only to Serve your Realization of Him. Once you are vowed to Him as His devotee, nothing can ever shake the depth of your "Bond" with Him, whether you wake, sleep, or dream, whether you live or die.

And so, do not waste this opportunity. Study this book. Read more about the Divine Life and Work of the Ruchira Avatar in His biography, *The Promised God-Man Is Here (The Extraordinary Life-Story, The "Crazy" Teaching-Work, and The Divinely "Emerging" World-Blessing Work Of The Divine World-Teacher Of The "Late-Time", Ruchira Avatar Adi Da Samraj)*, and in *See My Brightness Face to Face: A Celebration of the Ruchira Avatar, Adi Da Samraj, and the First Twenty-Five Years of His Divine Revelation Work.*[14] "Consider" the magnitude of what Avatar Adi Da has Done and the urgency of What He is Saying to you. And begin to participate in the greatest Grace that any human being can know—the Blessed life of joyful devotion and ecstatic service to the Divine Lord in Person, the Avatar of "Brightness", Adi Da Samraj.

Notes to
The All-Surpassing Revelation of the Divine World-Teacher, Ruchira Avatar Adi Da Samraj

1. By the word "Bright" (and its variations, such as "Brightness"), Avatar Adi Da refers to the eternally, infinitely, and inherently Self-Radiant Divine Being, the Being of Indivisible and Indestructible Light. (See also note 6, pp. 152-53.)

2. Avatar Adi Da uses the term "Real God" to indicate the True and Perfectly Subjective Source of all conditions, the True and Spiritual Divine Person, rather than any egoic (and, thus, false, or limited) presumptions about "God".

3. Avatar Adi Da Samraj is the "Avataric Incarnation", or the Divinely Descended Embodiment, of the Divine Person. The reference "Avataric Incarnation" indicates that Avatar Adi Da Samraj fulfills both the traditional expectation of the East—that the True God-Man is an Avatar, or an utterly Divine "Descent" of Real God in conditionally manifested form—and the traditional expectations of the West—that the True God-Man is an Incarnation, or an utterly human Embodiment of Real God.

4. B.V. Narasimha Swami and S. Subbarao, *Sage of Sakuri*, 4th ed. (Bombay: Shri B.T. Wagh, 1966), p. 204.

5. The term "radical" derives from the Latin "radix", meaning "root", and thus it principally means "irreducible", "fundamental", or "relating to the origin". In *The Dawn Horse Testament Of The Ruchira Avatar: The "Testament Of Secrets" Of The Divine World-Teacher, Ruchira Avatar Adi Da Samraj*, Avatar Adi Da defines "Radical" as "Gone To The Root, Core, Source, or Origin". Because Adi Da Samraj uses "radical" in this literal sense, it appears in quotation marks in His Wisdom-Teaching, in order to distinguish His usage from the common reference to an extreme (often political) view.

6. Avatar Adi Da uses the phrase "Most Perfect(ly)" in the sense of "Absolutely Perfect(ly)", indicating a reference to the seventh (or Divinely Enlightened) stage of life.

7. In Sanskrit, "Ruchira" means "bright, radiant, effulgent". The word "Tantra" (or "Tantric") does not merely indicate Spiritualized sexuality, as is the common presumption. Rather, it signifies "the inherent Unity that underlies and transcends all opposites, and that resolves all differences or distinctions".

In many of the Tantric traditions that have developed within both Hinduism and Buddhism, Tantric Adepts and aspirants use sexual

activity and intoxicating substances that are forbidden to more ortho-
dox or conventional practitioners. The Tantric's intention, however, is
never to merely indulge gross desires. The secret of the Tantric
approach is that it does not suppress, but rather employs and even
galvanizes, the passions and attachments of the body and mind, and
thus utilizes the most intense (and, therefore, also potentially most
deluding) energies of the being for the sake of Spiritual Realization.

"Sannyasin" is an ancient Sanskrit term for one who has
renounced all worldly "bonds" and who gives himself or herself completely to the Real-God-Realizing life.

The reference "Ruchira Tantric Sannyasin" indicates that Avatar
Adi Da Samraj is the Perfectly "Bright" ("Ruchira") One Who is Utterly
Free of all "bonds" to the conditional worlds ("Sannyasin"), and yet
never in any way dissociates from conditional existence ("Tantric"),
making skillful use of all the dimensions of conditional life in His
Divine Work of Liberation.

8. Avadhoot is a traditional term for one who has "shaken off" or
"passed beyond" all worldly attachments and cares, including all
motives of detachment (or conventional and other-worldly renunciation), all conventional notions of life and religion, and all seeking for
"answers" or "solutions" in the form of conditional experience or conditional knowledge. Therefore, "Divine Avadhoot", in reference to
Avatar Adi Da, indicates His Inherently Perfect Freedom as the One
Who Knows His Identity As the Divine Person and Who, thus, Always
Already Stands Free of the binding and deluding power of conditional
existence.

9. The total practice of the Way of Adidam is the full and complete
practice of the Way that Avatar Adi Da Samraj has Given to His devotees who are formal members of the first or the second congregation
of Adidam. One who embraces the total practice of the Way of Adidam conforms every aspect of his or her life and being to Avatar Adi
Da's Divine Word of Instruction. Therefore, it is only such devotees
(in the first or the second congregation of Adidam) who have the
potential of Realizing Divine Enlightenment.

10. The names and titles of the Ruchira Adidamas indicate their Realization and Spiritual significance in Avatar Adi Da's Work.

"Ruchira" and "Naitauba" both indicate membership in the
Ruchira Sannyasin Order. "Ruchira" is a title for all members of the
Ruchira Sannyasin Order who are practicing in the context of the
sixth stage of life, and indicates "a true devotee of the Ruchira Avatar,
the Da Avatar, the Love-Ananda Avatar, Adi Da Samraj, who is, by His
Grace, becoming Radiant, or 'Bright' with Love-Bliss, through

uniquely one-pointed (self-surrendering, self-forgetting, and self-transcending) feeling-Contemplation of Him, and, Thus and Thereby, of the True Divine Person" ["The Orders Of My True and Free Renunciate Devotees", in *The Lion Sutra—The Seventeen Companions Of The True Dawn Horse, Book Fifteen: The "Perfect Practice" Teachings For Formal Tantric Renunciates In The Divine Way Of Adidam*]. "Naitauba" is the traditional Fijian name for Adidam Samrajashram, the Great Island-Hermitage of Avatar Adi Da Samraj. As a general rule, all members of the Ruchira Sannyasin Order are to be formal residents of Adidam Samrajashram.

"Adidama" is composed of Avatar Adi Da's Principal Name "Adi Da" and the feminine indicator "Ma". In addition, in Sanskrit, "adi" means "first" and "dama" means "self-discipline". Therefore, the overall meaning of this title is "first among those who conform themselves to the Ruchira Avatar, Adi Da Samraj, by means of self-surrendering, self-forgetting, and self-transcending feeling-Contemplation of Him".

"Sukha" means "happiness, joy, delight" and "Dham" means "abode, dwelling". Therefore, as a personal renunciate name, "Sukha Dham" means "one who abides in happiness".

"Jangama" means "all living things", and "Hriddaya" is "heartfelt compassion, sympathy". Therefore, as a personal renunciate name, "Jangama Hriddaya" means "one who has heartfelt sympathy for all beings".

"Quandra" is a reference to the main female character in Avatar Adi Da's liturgical drama, *The Mummery*. Quandra is the embodiment of the Divine Goddess, or the Divine Spirit-Force. (*The Mummery— The Seventeen Companions Of The True Dawn Horse, Book Six: A Parable About Finding The Way To My House* is one of Avatar Adi Da's twenty-three "Source-Texts".)

"Adidama Quandra Mandala" is the "circle" ("Mandala") comprising the Ruchira Adidamas, Sukha Dham and Jangama Hriddaya. The Adidama Quandra Mandala is the first circle of Avatar Adi Da's devotees—those who stand closest to His bodily (human) Form in service and devotion.

11. The Name or Title "Bhagavan" is an ancient one used over the centuries for many Spiritual Realizers of the East. Its meanings in Sanskrit are "possessing fortune or wealth", "blessed", "holy". When applied to a great Spiritual Master, "Bhagavan" is understood to mean "bountiful God", or "Great God", or "Divine Lord".

The Name "Love-Ananda" combines both English ("Love") and Sanskrit ("Ananda", meaning "Bliss"), thus bridging the West and the East, and communicating Avatar Adi Da's Function as the Divine

World-Teacher. The combination of "Love" and "Ananda" means "the Divine Love-Bliss". The Name "Love-Ananda" was given to Avatar Adi Da by His principal human Spiritual Master, Swami Muktananda, who spontaneously conferred it upon Avatar Adi Da in 1969.

12. "Bhava" is a Sanskrit word traditionally used to refer to the enraptured feeling-swoon of Communion with the Divine.

13. *The Knee Of Listening*, chapter 3.

14. Both books are available from the Dawn Horse Press (see p. 213 for ordering information).

The Divine Scripture of Adidam

*The Full and Final Word of
The Divine World-Teacher,
Ruchira Avatar Adi Da Samraj,
Given in His Twenty-Three "Source-Texts"
of "Bright" Divine Self-Revelation
and Perfect Heart-Instruction*

The twenty-three "Source-Texts" of the Ruchira Avatar are the most extraordinary books ever written. They are the world's greatest Treasure, the Ultimate and All-Completing Revelation of Truth.

These books are the unmediated Word of the Very Divine Person, Adi Da Samraj, Who is Offering the True World-Religion of Adidam, the Religion of Most Perfect Divine Enlightenment, or Indivisible Oneness with Real God. Avatar Adi Da Samraj is the Realizer, the Revealer, and the Divine Author of all that is Written in these sublime Texts. No mind can begin to comprehend the Magnificent Self-Revelations and Self-Confessions Given by Adi Da Samraj in these books. And these twenty-three "Source-Texts" (together with the "Supportive Texts", in which Avatar Adi Da Gives further detailed Instruction relative to the functional, practical, relational, and cultural disciplines of the Way of Adidam[1]) Give Avatar Adi Da's complete Instruction in the Process (never before Known or Revealed in its entirety) of Most Perfectly Realizing Reality Itself, or Truth Itself, or Real God.

---

1. The functional, practical, relational, and cultural disciplines of Adidam are described in brief on pp. 196-200 of this book. Among Avatar Adi Da's "Supportive Texts" are included such books as *Conscious Exercise and the Transcendental Sun*, *The Eating Gorilla Comes in Peace*, *Love of the Two-Armed Form*, and *Easy Death*. (New editions of the first three of these "Supportive Texts" are in preparation.)

The long-existing religious traditions of the world have depended on oral traditions and memory. Their teachings and disciplines typically developed long after the death of their founders, based on the remembered (and often legendary or mythological) deeds and instruction of those Realizers. These traditions have thus been colored by legends and cultural influences that obscure the original revelation. Yet, every historical revelation, even in its first purity, has necessarily been limited by the degree of realization of its founder. Adidam does not depend on the vagaries of oral tradition and memory, nor is it limited by any partial point of view. Adidam is the Perfect Divine Way Revealed by the One Who Is Reality Itself (or Truth Itself, or Real God). Adi Da Samraj is alive now in bodily (human) Form, and He has Personally tested the entire course of Divine Enlightenment described in these books in the course of His own human Lifetime.

In His twenty-three "Source-Texts", Avatar Adi Da is Speaking to all humankind, asking us to feel our actual situation, to take seriously the mayhem of the world, its pain and dissatisfaction, its terrible potential for suffering. And, with Divine Passion, He Calls every one to turn to Him and, in that turning, to rise out of gross struggle and conflict. The twenty-three "Source-Texts" of Avatar Adi Da Samraj Reveal the greater Purpose and Destiny of humanity. Indeed, they are the key to the very survival of this planet. This unparalleled body of Scripture is the Message you have always been waiting for and never imagined could come.

In the Words of the Divine Avatar Himself:

"All the Scriptures are now fulfilled in your sight, and your prayers are answered with a clear voice."

In *The Dawn Horse Testament*, Avatar Adi Da Samraj makes His own Confession relative to His Impulse in creating His twenty-three "Source-Texts", and He also expresses the requirement He places on all His devotees to make His Divine Word available to all:

Now I Have, By All My "Crazy" Means, Revealed The One and Many Secrets Of The Great Person Of The Heart. For Your Sake, I Made My Every Work and Word. And Now, By Every Work and Word I Made, I Have Entirely Confessed (and Showed) My Self, and Always Freely, and Even As A Free Man, In The "Esoteric" Language Of Intimacy and Ecstasy, Openly Worded To You (and To all). Even Now (and Always), By This (My Word Of Heart), I Address every Seeming Separate being (and each one As The Heart Itself), Because It Is Necessary That all beings, Even The Entire Cosmic Domain Of Seeming Separate beings, Be (In all times and places) Called To Wisdom and The Heart.

The Twenty-Three "Source-Texts" of Avatar Adi Da Samraj

The twenty-three "Source-Texts" of Avatar Adi Da Samraj include: (1) an opening series of five books on the fundamentals of the Way of Adidam (*The Five Books Of The Heart Of The Adidam Revelation*), (2) an extended series of seventeen books covering the principal aspects of the Way of Adidam in detail (*The Seventeen Companions Of The True Dawn Horse*), and (3) Avatar Adi Da's paramount "Source-Text" summarizing the entire course of the Way of Adidam (*The Dawn Horse Testament*).

The Five Books Of The Heart Of The Adidam Revelation

Aham Da Asmi
(Beloved, I Am Da)

The Five Books Of The Heart Of The Adidam Revelation, Book One: The "Late-Time" Avataric Revelation Of The True and Spiritual Divine Person (The egoless Personal Presence Of Reality and Truth, Which Is The Only Real God)

Ruchira Avatara Gita
(The Way Of The Divine Heart-Master)

The Five Books Of The Heart Of The Adidam Revelation,
Book Two: The "Late-Time" Avataric Revelation Of
The Great Secret Of The Divinely Self-Revealed Way
That Most Perfectly Realizes The True and Spiritual
Divine Person (The egoless Personal Presence Of
Reality and Truth, Which Is The Only Real God)

Da Love-Ananda Gita
(The Free Gift Of The Divine Love-Bliss)

The Five Books Of The Heart Of The Adidam Revelation,
Book Three: The "Late-Time" Avataric Revelation Of
The Great Means To Worship and To Realize
The True and Spiritual Divine Person
(The egoless Personal Presence Of Reality and Truth,
Which Is The Only Real God)

Hridaya Rosary
(Four Thorns Of Heart-Instruction)

The Five Books Of The Heart Of The Adidam Revelation,
Book Four: The "Late-Time" Avataric Revelation Of
The Universally Tangible Divine Spiritual Body,
Which Is The Supreme Agent Of The Great Means
To Worship and To Realize The True and Spiritual
Divine Person (The egoless Personal Presence Of
Reality and Truth, Which Is The Only Real God)

Eleutherios
(The Only Truth That Sets The Heart Free)

The Five Books Of The Heart Of The Adidam Revelation,
Book Five: The "Late-Time" Avataric Revelation Of The
"Perfect Practice" Of The Great Means To Worship and
To Realize The True and Spiritual Divine Person
(The egoless Personal Presence Of Reality and Truth,
Which Is The Only Real God)

The Seventeen Companions
Of The True Dawn Horse

Real God *Is* The Indivisible Oneness
Of Unbroken Light

*The Seventeen Companions Of The True Dawn Horse,
Book One: Reality, Truth, and The "Non-Creator" God
In The True World-Religion Of Adidam*

The Truly Human New World-Culture
Of *Unbroken* Real-God-Man

*The Seventeen Companions Of The True Dawn Horse,
Book Two: The *Eastern* Versus The *Western* Traditional
Cultures Of Mankind, and The Unique New *Non-Dual*
Culture Of The True World-Religion Of Adidam*

The *Only* Complete Way To Realize
The Unbroken Light Of *Real* God

*The Seventeen Companions Of The True Dawn Horse,
Book Three: An Introductory Overview Of The "Radical"
Divine Way Of The True World-Religion Of Adidam*

The Knee Of Listening

*The Seventeen Companions Of The True Dawn Horse,
Book Four: The Early-Life Ordeal and The "Radical"
Spiritual Realization Of The Ruchira Avatar*

The Method Of The Ruchira Avatar

*The Seventeen Companions Of The True Dawn Horse,
Book Five: The Divine Way Of Adidam Is
An ego-Transcending *Relationship*,
Not An ego-Centric Technique*

The Mummery

*The Seventeen Companions Of The True Dawn Horse,
Book Six: A Parable About Finding The Way To *My* House*

He-and-She Is Me

*The Seventeen Companions Of The True Dawn Horse,
Book Seven: The Indivisibility Of Consciousness and Light
In The Divine Body Of The Ruchira Avatar*

Divine Spiritual Baptism
Versus Cosmic Spiritual Baptism

*The Seventeen Companions Of The True Dawn Horse,
Book Eight: Divine Hridaya-Shakti Versus
Cosmic Kundalini Shakti In The Divine Way Of Adidam*

Ruchira Tantra Yoga

*The Seventeen Companions Of The True Dawn Horse,
Book Nine: The Physical-Spiritual (and Truly Religious)
Method Of Mental, Emotional, Sexual, and Whole Bodily
Health and Enlightenment In The Divine Way Of Adidam*

The Seven Stages Of Life

*The Seventeen Companions Of The True Dawn Horse,
Book Ten: Transcending The Six Stages Of egoic Life
and Realizing The ego-Transcending Seventh Stage Of Life,
In The Divine Way Of Adidam*

The All-Completing and Final
Divine Revelation To Mankind

*The Seventeen Companions Of The True Dawn Horse,
Book Eleven: A Summary Description
Of The Supreme Yoga Of The Seventh Stage Of Life
In The Divine Way Of Adidam*

The Heart Of The Dawn Horse Testament
Of The Ruchira Avatar

*The Seventeen Companions Of The True Dawn Horse,
Book Twelve: The Epitome Of The "Testament Of Secrets"
Of The Divine World-Teacher,
Ruchira Avatar Adi Da Samraj*

What, Where, When, How, Why, and <u>Who</u> To Remember To Be Happy

*The Seventeen Companions Of The True Dawn Horse,
Book Thirteen: A Simple Explanation Of The Divine Way
Of Adidam (For Children, and <u>Everyone</u> Else)*

Santosha Adidam

*The Seventeen Companions Of The True Dawn Horse,
Book Fourteen: The Essential Summary
Of The Divine Way Of Adidam*

The Lion Sutra

*The Seventeen Companions Of The True Dawn Horse,
Book Fifteen: The "Perfect Practice" Teachings For Formal
Tantric Renunciates In The Divine Way Of Adidam*

The Overnight Revelation Of Conscious Light

*The Seventeen Companions Of The True Dawn Horse,
Book Sixteen: The "My House" Discourses
On The Indivisible Tantra Of Adidam*

The Basket Of Tolerance

*The Seventeen Companions Of The True Dawn Horse,
Book Seventeen: The Perfect Guide To Perfectly <u>Unified</u>
Understanding Of The One and Great Tradition
Of Mankind, and Of The Divine Way Of Adidam
As The Perfect <u>Completing</u> Of The One
and Great Tradition Of Mankind*

The Dawn Horse Testament

The Dawn Horse Testament Of The Ruchira Avatar

*The "Testament Of Secrets" Of The Divine World-Teacher,
Ruchira Avatar Adi Da Samraj*

The Song Of Perfect Love-Bliss

An Introduction to the Da Love-Ananda Gita

This extraordinary Revelation-Text is the Joyous Song (or "Gita", in Sanskrit) of Happiness, Freedom, and Love-Bliss (or "Love-Ananda"). And Its Great Singer is the True and Spiritual Divine Person, Manifested by man-Born Descent as the Divine World-Teacher, Ruchira Avatar Adi Da Samraj.

"Love-Ananda" is one of Ruchira Avatar Adi Da's Divine Names. It uniquely communicates His Embrace of all beings—East and West—by uniting the English word "Love" and the Sanskrit word "Ananda". The Divine World-Teacher Declares, in His *Da Love-Ananda Gita*, that He Is "Love-Ananda", He Is "the Very Person of the 'Bright' Divine Love-Bliss".

Inherent in every being is a movement toward Love-Bliss. But that desire for Happiness is frustrated by the many obvious limitations of conditional existence. Every one dies, every one suffers, all apparent pleasures are merely temporary distractions from inevitable mortality. This reality has led many who have considered such matters deeply to seek to go beyond the desire for pleasure and to seek Happiness, or Love-Bliss, apart from the mortal life. Indeed, this is the usual basis of all religious and Spiritual endeavor. However, Avatar Adi Da Love-Ananda has Revealed that all seeking is ultimately fruitless—because it is a denial of Reality Itself, Which Is Happiness Itself.

In Part One of the *Da Love-Ananda Gita*, "The Search for Truth Is Absurd and Unnecessary", Avatar Adi Da Love-Ananda Speaks about the true origin of suffering while Revealing the Heart-Instruction implicit in His Name:

AVATAR ADI DA SAMRAJ: Love-Bliss Is Reality Itself. If you withdraw from Love-Bliss, or if you withhold yourself from Love-Bliss, or if you deny Love-Bliss, or if you merely seek Love-Bliss—you, inevitably (and by that very act), suffer. . . . If you withdraw from My always present-time Divine Self-Revelation (or Divine Self-Manifestation) of Love-Bliss, you suffer. Therefore, do not withdraw from Me, and do not seek Me, but, simply (devotionally), recognize Me, and (by that simple devotional recognition) be devotionally responsive to Me, always Love-Bliss-"Bright", Divinely Self-Revealed before you.

The one hundred and eight verses of Part Two form the principal Text of the *Da Love-Ananda Gita*. In these verses, Avatar Adi Da Love-Ananda Sings the Miraculous Revelation that Real God—the Ultimate Source and Nature and Person of all and All—is Realizable. To Give this Gift of Real-God-Realization is the very Purpose of His Avataric Incarnation during this "late-time" of dark despair. Avatar Adi Da Love-Ananda is Himself the Great Means, the Sublime Gift, and the Perfect Realization of the Eternal "Bright" Divine Self-Condition. Realization of Avatar Adi Da Love-Ananda is Realization of Perfect Love-Bliss—the only True Freedom.

This *Da Love-Ananda Gita* is the fundamental Instruction Ruchira Avatar Adi Da Gives to all who formally embrace the Real-God-Realizing Way of Adidam. For all congregations[1] and for all stages of practice in the Way of Adidam, the foundation Principle is always the same—it is the simple and direct practice known as "Ruchira Avatara Bhakti Yoga".

Ruchira Avatara Bhakti Yoga is the Spiritual discipline (or "Yoga") of devotion (or "Bhakti") to the Ruchira Avatar, Adi Da Love-Ananda Samraj. Ruchira Avatara Bhakti Yoga is effectively practiced only in active response to the Gift

---

1. For a description of the congregations of Adidam please see pp. 184-95.

of devotionally recognizing Ruchira Avatar Adi Da <u>As</u> Real God. That devotional recognition and responsive practice is the foundation of the esoteric Process of Real-God-Realization—it is the very Means by which Ruchira Avatar Adi Da's Realization is, ultimately, duplicated in His every devotee.

Part Three of the *Da Love-Ananda Gita*, "Ruchira Avatara Bhakti Sara (The Essence of Devotion to Me)", consists of fifty-four brief verses, in which Avatar Adi Da Love-Ananda summarizes the right and effective practice of the Divinely Revealed Yoga of Ruchira Avatara Bhakti.

Finally, in the ecstatic Epilogue to the *Da Love-Ananda Gita*, "What Will You Do If You Love Me?", Avatar Adi Da Love-Ananda Calls forth the love-response of all who truly turn to Him, through His Divinely "Intoxicated" (and Divinely "Intoxicating")[2] Speech.

Altogether, the *Da Love-Ananda Gita* is Avatar Adi Da Love-Ananda's Perfect Revelation and direct Offering to you and to all beings of the simplest and only complete Way of Love-Bliss-Happiness.

---

2. In this case, "intoxicated" (or "intoxicating") is not referring to a common intoxicant such as alcohol, but of a Spiritual "Intoxicant"—by means of which devotees of Avatar Adi Da are Drawn beyond the usual egoic self through the Blessing Grace and Siddhis of Avatar Adi Da into a state of devotional Communion (and, ultimately, of Identification) with Him.

DA LOVE-ANANDA GITA

(THE FREE GIFT OF THE DIVINE LOVE-BLISS)

RUCHIRA AVATAR ADI DA SAMRAJ
Adidam Samrajashram (Naitauba), Fiji, 1997

Do Not Misunderstand <u>Me</u>—
I Am <u>Not</u> "Within" <u>you</u>,
but you <u>Are</u> In <u>Me</u>,
and I Am <u>Not</u> a Mere "Man"
in the "Middle" of Mankind,
but All of Mankind Is Surrounded,
and Pervaded, and Blessed By <u>Me</u>

This Essay has been written by Avatar Adi Da Samraj as His Personal Introduction to each volume of His "Source-Texts". Its purpose is to help you to understand His great Confessions rightly, and not interpret His Words from a conventional point of view, as limited cultic statements made by an ego. His Description of what "cultism" <u>really</u> is is an astounding and profound Critique of mankind's entire religious, scientific, and social search. In "First Word", Avatar Adi Da is directly inviting you to inspect and relinquish the ego's motive to glorify itself and to refuse What is truly Great. Only by understanding this fundamental ego-fault can one really receive the Truth that Adi Da Samraj Reveals in this Book and in His Wisdom-Teaching altogether. And it is because this fault is so engrained and so largely unconscious that Avatar Adi Da has placed "First Word" at the beginning of each of His "Source-Texts", so that, each time you begin to read one of His twenty-three "Source-Texts", you may be refreshed and strengthened in your understanding of the right orientation and approach to Him and His Heart-Word.

Yes! There is <u>no</u> religion, <u>no</u> Way of God, <u>no</u> Way of Divine Realization, <u>no</u> Way of Enlightenment, and <u>no</u> Way of Liberation that is Higher or Greater than Truth Itself. Indeed, there is <u>no</u> religion, <u>no</u> science, <u>no</u> man or woman, <u>no</u> conditionally manifested being of any kind, no world (any "where"), and no "God" (or "God"-Idea) that is Higher or Greater than Truth Itself.

Therefore, no ego-"I"[1] (or presumed separate, and, necessarily, actively separative, and, at best, only Truth-seeking, being or "thing") is (itself) Higher or Greater than Truth Itself. And no ego-"I" is (itself) even Equal to Truth Itself. And no ego-"I" is (itself) even (now, or ever) Able to Realize Truth Itself—because, necessarily, Truth (Itself) Inherently Transcends (or Is That Which Is Higher and Greater than) every one (himself or herself) and every "thing" (itself). Therefore, it is only in the transcending (or the "radical"[2] Process of Going Beyond the root, the cause, and the act) of egoity itself (or of presumed separateness, and of performed separativeness, and of even all ego-based seeking for Truth Itself) that Truth (Itself) Is Realized (As It Is, Utterly Beyond the ego-"I" itself).

Truth (Itself) Is That Which Is Always Already The Case. That Which Is The Case (Always, and Always Already) Is (necessarily) Reality. Therefore, Reality (Itself) Is Truth, and Reality (Itself) Is the Only Truth.

Reality (Itself) Is the Only, and, necessarily, Non-Separate, or All-and-all-Including, and All-and-all-Transcending, One and "What" That Is. Because It Is All and all, and because It Is (Also) That Which Transcends (or Is Higher and Greater than) All and all, Reality (Itself), Which Is Truth (Itself), or That Which Is The Case (Always, and Always Already), Is the One and Only Real God. Therefore, Reality (Itself) Is (necessarily) the One and Great Subject of true religion, and Reality (Itself) Is (necessarily) the One and Great Way of Real God, Real (and True) Divine Realization, Real (and, necessarily, Divine) En-Light-enment, and Real (and, necessarily, Divine) Liberation (from all egoity, all separateness, all separativeness, all fear, and all heartlessness).

Notes to *First Word* can be found on pp. 62-65.

The <u>only</u> true religion is the religion that <u>Realizes</u> Truth. The <u>only</u> true science is the science that <u>Knows</u> Truth. The <u>only</u> true man or woman (or being of any kind) is one that <u>Surrenders</u> to Truth. The only true world is one that <u>Embodies</u> Truth. And the only True (and <u>Real</u>) God Is the One Reality (or Condition of Being) That <u>Is</u> Truth. Therefore, <u>Reality</u> (Itself), Which Is the One and Only Truth, and (therefore, necessarily) the One and Only Real God, <u>must</u> become (or be made) the constantly applied Measure of religion, and of science, and of the world itself, and of even <u>all</u> of the life (and <u>all</u> of the mind) of Man—or else religion, and science, and the world itself, and even any and every sign of Man <u>inevitably</u> (all, and together) become a pattern of illusions, a mere (and even terrible) "problem", the very (and even principal) cause of human seeking, and the perpetual cause of contentious human strife. Indeed, if religion, and science, and the world itself, and the total life (and the total mind) of Man are not Surrendered and Aligned to Reality (Itself), and, Thus, Submitted to be Measured (or made Lawful) by Truth (Itself), and, Thus, Given to the truly devotional (and, thereby, truly ego-transcending) Realization of <u>That</u> Which Is the <u>Only</u> <u>Real</u> God—then, in the presumed "knowledge" of mankind, Reality (Itself), and Truth (Itself), and <u>Real</u> God (or the One and Only Existence, or Being, or Person That <u>Is</u>) <u>ceases</u> <u>to</u> <u>Exist</u>.

Aham Da Asmi.[3] Beloved, I <u>Am</u> Da, the One and Only Person Who <u>Is</u>, the Eternally Self-Existing, and Eternally Self-Radiant,[4] or "Bright",[5] Person of Love-Bliss, the One and Only and (necessarily) Divine Self (or Inherently Non-Separate, and, therefore, Inherently egoless, Self-Condition and Source-Condition) of one and of all and of All. I Am Self-Manifesting (now, and forever hereafter) <u>As</u> the Ruchira Avatar, Adi Da Samraj. I <u>Am</u> the Ruchira Avatar, Adi Da Samraj, the Avataric Realizer, the Avataric Revealer, the Avataric Incarnation, and the Avataric Revelation of Reality <u>Itself</u>.[6] I <u>Am</u> the Avatarically Incarnate Realizer, the

43

Avatarically Incarnate Revealer, and the Avatarically Incarnate Revelation of the One and Only Reality, Which Is the One and Only Truth, and Which Is the One and Only <u>Real</u> God. I <u>Am</u> the Great Realizer, Revealer, and Revelation long-Promised (and long-Expected) for the "late-time", <u>this</u> (now, and forever hereafter) time, the "dark" epoch of mankind's "Great Forgetting"[7] (and, <u>potentially</u>, the Great Epoch of mankind's Perpetual Remembering) of Reality, of Truth, of Real God, Which Is the Great, True, and Spiritual Divine Person (or the One and Non-Separate and Indivisible Source-Condition and Self-Condition) of all and All.

Beloved, I <u>Am</u> Da, the Divine Giver, the Giver (of All That I <u>Am</u>) to one and to all and to the All of all—now, and forever hereafter, here, and every "where" in the Cosmic domain. Therefore, for the Purpose of Revealing the Way of <u>Real</u> God, or of Real and True Divine Realization, and in order to Divinely En-Light-en and Divinely Liberate all and All, I Am (Uniquely, Completely, and Most Perfectly[8]) Revealing My Divine and Very Person (and "Bright" Self-Condition) to all and All, by Means of My Divine Self-Manifestation, <u>As</u> (and by Means of) the Ruchira Avatar, Adi Da Samraj.

In My Divine Self-Manifestation As the Ruchira Avatar, Adi Da Samraj, I <u>Am</u> the Divine Secret, the Divine Revelation of the <u>Esoteric</u> Truth, the Direct, and all-Completing, and all-Unifying Revelation of <u>Real</u> God.

My Divine Self-Confessions and My Divine Teaching-Revelations Are <u>the</u> Great (Final, and all-Completing, and all-Unifying) <u>Esoteric</u> Revelation to mankind, and <u>not</u> a merely <u>exoteric</u>, or conventionally religious, or even ordinary Spiritual, or ego-made, or so-called "cultic", communication to public (or merely social) ears.

The greatest opportunity, and the greatest responsibility, of My devotees is Satsang[9] with Me, Which is to live in the Condition of self-surrendering, self-forgetting, and, always more and more, self-transcending devotional relationship to Me, and, Thus and Thereby, to Realize the

Condition of the Divine Heart, the Condition of the Divine Person, Which Is the Divine and Non-Separate Self-Condition, and Source-Condition, of all and All, and Which Is Self-Existing and Self-Radiant Consciousness Itself, but Which is not separate in or as any one (or any "thing") at all. Therefore, My essential Gift to one and all is this Satsang with Me. And My essential Work with one and all is Satsang-Work, to Live (and to Be Merely Present) As the Divine Heart among My devotees.

The only-by-Me Revealed and Given Way of Adidam (Which is the only-by-Me Revealed and Given Way of the Heart, or the only-by-Me Revealed and Given Way of "Radical Understanding"[10]) is the Way of Satsang with Me—the devotionally Me-recognizing[11] and devotionally to-Me-responding practice (and ego-transcending self-discipline) of living in My constant Divine Company, such that the relationship with Me becomes the Real (and constant) Condition of life. Fundamentally, this Satsang with Me is the one thing done by My devotees. Because the only-by-Me Revealed and Given Way of Adidam is always (in every present-time moment) a directly ego-transcending and Really Me-Finding practice, the otherwise constant (and burdensome) tendency to seek is not exploited in this Satsang with Me. And the essential work of the community of the four formal congregations of My devotees[12] is to make ego-transcending Satsang with Me available to all others.

Everything that serves the availability of Satsang with Me is (now, and forever hereafter) the responsibility of the four formal congregations of My formally practicing devotees. I am not here to publicly "promote" this Satsang with Me. In the intimate circumstances of their humanly expressed devotional love of Me, I Speak My Divinely Self-Revealing Word to My devotees, and they (because of their devotional response to Me) bring My Divinely Self-Revealing Word to all others. Therefore, even though I am not (and have never been, and never will be) a "public"

Teacher (or a broadly publicly active, and conventionally socially conformed, "religious figure"), My devotees function fully and freely (as My devotees) in the daily public world of ordinary life.

I Always Already Stand Free. Therefore, I have always (in My Avataric-Incarnation-Work) Stood Free, in the traditional "Crazy" (and non-conventional, or spontaneous and non-"public") Manner,[13] in order to Guarantee the Freedom, the Uncompromising Rightness, and the Fundamental Integrity of My Teaching (Work and Word), and in order to Freely and Fully and Fully Effectively Perform My universal Blessing Work. I Am Present (now, and forever hereafter) to Divinely Serve, Divinely En-Light-en, and Divinely Liberate those who accept the Eternal Vow and all the life-responsibilities (or the full and complete practice)[14] associated with the only-by-Me Revealed and Given Way of Adidam. Because I Am Thus Given to My formally and fully practicing devotees, I do not Serve a "public" role, and I do not Work in a "public" (or even a merely "institutionalized") manner. Nevertheless, now, and forever hereafter, I constantly Bless all beings, and this entire world, and the total Cosmic domain. And all who feel My universally Given Blessing, and who recognize Me with true devotional love, are (Thus) Called to resort to Me, but only if they approach Me in the traditional devotional manner, as responsibly practicing (and truly ego-surrendering, and rightly Me-serving) members (or, in some, unique, cases, as invited guests) of one or the other of the four formal congregations of My formally practicing devotees.

I expect this formal discipline of right devotional approach to Me to have been freely and happily embraced by every one who would enter into My Company. The natural human reason for this is that there is a potential liability inherent in all human associations. And the root and nature of that potential liability is the ego, or the active human presumption of separateness, and the ego-act of human separativeness. Therefore, in order that the liabilities of egoity are understood, and voluntarily and responsibly disciplined, by those who approach Me, I require demonstrated right devotion, based on really effective self-understanding and truly heart-felt recognition-response to Me, as the basis for any one's right to enter into My Company. And, in this manner, not only the egoic tendency, but also the tendency toward religious "cultism", is constantly undermined in the only-by-Me Revealed and Given Way of Adidam.

Because people appear within this human condition, this simultaneously attractive and frightening "dream" world, they tend to live (and to interpret both the conditional, or cosmic and psycho-physical, reality and the Unconditional, or Divine, Reality) from the "point of view" of this apparent, and bewildering, mortal human condition. And, because of this universal human bewilderment, and the ongoing human reaction to the threatening force of mortal life-events, there is an even ancient ritual that all human beings rather unconsciously (or automatically, and without discriminative understanding) desire and tend to repeatedly (and under all conditions) enact. Therefore, wherever you see an association of human beings gathered for any purpose (or around any idea, or symbol, or person, or subject of any kind), the same human bewilderment-ritual is tending to be enacted by one and all.

Human beings always tend to encircle (and, thereby, to contain, and, ultimately, to entrap and abuse, or even to blithely ignore) the presumed "center" of their lives—a book, a person, a symbol, an idea, or whatever. They tend to encircle the "center" (or the "middle"), and they tend to seek to exclusively acquire all "things" (or all power of control) for the circle (or toward the "middle") of themselves. In this manner, the group becomes an ego ("inward"-directed, or separate and separative)—just as the individual body-mind becomes, by self-referring self-contraction, the separate and separative ego-"I" ("inward"-

directed, or ego-centric, and exclusively acquiring all "things", or all power of control, for itself). Thus, by <u>self-contraction</u> upon the presumed "center" of their lives, human beings, in their collective ego-centricity, make "cults" (or bewildered and frightened "centers" of power, and control, and exclusion) in <u>every</u> area of life.

Anciently, the "cult"-making process was done, most especially, in the political and social sphere—and religion was, as even now, mostly an exoteric, or political and social, exercise that was <u>always</u> used to legitimize (or, otherwise, to "de-throne") political and social "authority-figures". Anciently, the cyclically (or even annually) culminating product of this exoteric religio-political "cult" was the ritual "de-throning" (or ritual deposition) of the one in the "middle" (just as, even in these times, political leaders are periodically "deposed", by elections, by rules of term and succession, by scandal, by slander, by force, and so on).

Traditional societies, everywhere throughout the ancient world, made and performed this annual (or otherwise periodic) religio-political "cult" ritual. The ritual of "en-throning" and "de-throning" was a reflection of the human observation of the annual cycle of the seasons of the natural world, and the same ritual was a reflection of the human concern and effort to <u>control</u> the signs potential in the cycle of the natural world, in order to ensure human survival (through control of weather, harvests and every kind of "fate", or even every fraction of existence upon which human beings depend for both survival and pleasure, or psycho-physical well-being). Indeed, the motive behind the ancient agrarian (and, later, urbanized, or universalized) ritual of the one in the "middle" was, essentially, the same motive that, in the modern era, takes the form of the culture of scientific materialism (and even all of the modern culture of materialistic "realism")—it is the motive to gain, and to maintain, <u>control</u>, and the effort to control even everything and everyone (via both knowledge and gross power). Thus, the ritualized (or bewildered yes/no, or desire/fear) life of mankind in the modern era is, essentially, the same as that of mankind in the ancient days.

In the ancient ritual of "en-throning" and "de-throning", the person (or subject) in the "middle" was ritually mocked, abused, deposed, and banished—and a new person (or subject) was installed in the "center" of the religio-political "cult". In the equivalent modern ritual of dramatized ambiguity relative to everything and everyone (and, perhaps especially, "authority-figures"), the person (or symbol, or idea) in the "middle" (or that which is given power by means of popular fascination) is first "cultified" (or made much of), and then, progressively, doubted, mocked, and abused, until, at last, all the negative emotions are (by culturally and socially ritualized dramatization) dissolved, the "middle" (having thus ceased to be fascinating) is abandoned, and a "new" person (or symbol, or idea) becomes the subject of popular fascination (only to be reduced, eventually, to the same "cultic" ritual, or cycle of "rise" and "fall").

Just as in <u>every</u> other area of human life, the tendency of <u>all</u> those who, in the modern era, would become involved in religious or Spiritual life is also to make a "cult", a circle that ever increases its separate and separative dimensions, beginning from the "center", surrounding it, perhaps even, ultimately, controlling it to the degree that it altogether ceases to be effective (or even interesting). Such "cultism" is ego-based, and ego-reinforcing, and, no matter how "esoteric" it presumes itself to be, it is (as in the ancient setting) entirely exoteric, or, at least, more and more limited to (and by) merely social and gross physical activities and conditions.

The form that every "cult" imitates is the pattern of egoity (or the ego-"I") itself, the presumed "middle" of every ordinary individual life. It is the self-contraction, the avoidance of relationship, which "creates" the fearful sense of separate mind, and all the endless habits and motives of egoic desire, or bewildered (and self-deluded) seeking. It is what is, ordinarily, called (or presumed to be) the real and necessary and only "life".

From birth, the human being (by reaction to the blows and limits of psycho-physical existence) begins to presume separate existence to be his or her very nature, and, on that basis, the human individual spends his or her entire life generating and serving a circle of ownership (or self-protecting acquisition) all around the ego-"I". The egoic motive encloses all the other beings it can acquire, all the "things" it can acquire, all the states and thoughts it can acquire—all the possible emblems, symbols, experiences, and sensations it can possibly acquire. Therefore, when any human being begins to involve himself or herself in some religious or Spiritual association, or, for that matter, any extension of his or her own subjectivity, he or she tends again to "create" that same circle about a "center".

The "cult" (whether of religion, or of politics, or of science, or of popular culture) is a dramatization of egoity, of separativeness, even of the entrapment and betrayal of the "center" (or the "middle"), by one and all. Therefore, I have always Refused to assume the role and the position of the "man in the middle"—and I have always, from the beginning of My formal Teaching and Blessing Work, Criticized, Resisted, and Shouted About the "cultic" (or ego-based, and ego-reinforcing, and merely "talking" and "believing", and not understanding and not really practicing) "school" (or tendency) of ordinary religious and Spiritual life. Indeed, true Satsang with Me (or the true devotional relationship to Me) is an always (and specifically, and intensively) anti-"cultic", or truly non-"cultic", Process.

The true devotional relationship to Me is not separative, or merely "inward"-directed, nor is It about attachment to Me as a mere (and, necessarily, limited) human being (or a "man in the middle")—for, if My devotee indulges in ego-bound (or self-referring and self-serving) attachment to Me as a mere human "other", My Divine Nature (and, therefore, the Divine Nature of Reality Itself) is not (as the very Basis for religious and Spiritual practice in My Company) truly devotionally recognized and rightly devotionally acknowledged, and, if such non-recognition of Me is the case, there is no truly ego-transcending devotional response to My Divine Presence and Person, and, thus, such presumed-to-be "devotion" to Me is not Divine Communion, and such presumed-to-be "devotion" to Me is not Divinely Liberating. Therefore, because the true devotional (and, thus, truly devotionally Me-recognizing and truly devotionally to-Me-responding) relationship to Me is entirely a counter-egoic (and truly and only Divine) discipline, It does not tend to become a "cult" (or, otherwise, to support the "cultic" tendency of Man).

The true devotional practice of true Satsang with Me is (inherently) expansive, or relational, and the self-contracting (or separate and separative) self-"center" is neither Its motive nor Its source. In true Satsang with Me, the egoic "center" is always already undermined as a "center" (or a presumed separate, and actively separative, entity). The Principle of true Satsang with Me is Me, Beyond (and not "within", or otherwise supporting) the ego-"I".

True Satsang with Me is the true "Round Dance" of Esoteric Spirituality. I am not trapped in the "middle" of My devotees. I "Dance" in the "Round" with each and every one of My devotees. I "Dance" in the circle, and, therefore, I am not merely a "motionless man" in the "middle". At the true "Center" (or the Divine Heart), I Am— Beyond definition (or separateness). I Am the Indivisible (or Most Perfectly Prior, Inherently Non-Separate, Inherently egoless, or centerless, boundless, and, necessarily, Divine) Consciousness (Itself) and the Indivisible (or Most Perfectly Prior, Inherently Non-Separate, Inherently egoless, or centerless, boundless, and, necessarily, Divine) Light (Itself). I Am the Very Being and the Very Presence (or Self-Radiance) of Self-Existing and Eternally Unqualified (or Non-"Different"[15]) Consciousness (Itself).

In the "Round Dance" of true Satsang with Me (or of

right and true devotional relationship to Me), I (My Self) Am Communicated directly to every one who lives in heart-felt relationship with Me (insofar as each one feels, <u>Beyond</u> the ego-"I" of body-mind, to <u>Me</u>). Therefore, I am not the mere "man" (or the separate human, or psycho-physical, one), and I am not merely "in the middle" (or separated out, and limited, and confined, by egoic seekers). I <u>Am</u> the One (and all-Transcending) Person of Reality Itself, Non-Separate, never merely at the egoic "center" (or "in the middle", or "<u>within</u>", and "inward" to, the egoic body-mind of My any devotee), but always <u>with</u> each one (and all), and always in relationship with each one (and all), and always Beyond each one (and all).

Therefore, My devotee is not Called, by Me, merely to turn "inward" (or upon the ego-"I"), or to struggle and seek to survive merely as a self-contracted and self-referring and self-seeking and self-serving ego-"center". Instead, I Call My devotee to turn the heart (and the total body-mind) <u>toward</u> Me (all-and-All-Surrounding, and all-and-All-Pervading), <u>in</u> <u>relationship</u>, <u>Beyond</u> the body-mind-self of My devotee (and <u>not</u> <u>merely</u> "<u>within</u>", or contained and containable "within" the separate, separative, and self-contracted domain of the body-mind-self, or the ego-"I", of My would-be devotee). I Call My devotee to function freely, My Light and My Person always (and under all circumstances) presumed and experienced (and not merely sought). Therefore, true Satsang with Me is the Real Company of Truth, or of Reality Itself (Which <u>Is</u> the Only Real God). True Satsang with Me Serves life, because I Move (or Radiate) into life. I always Contact life in relationship.

I do not Call My devotees to become absorbed into a "cultic" gang of exoteric and ego-centric religionists. I certainly Call <u>all</u> My devotees to cooperative community (or, otherwise, to fully cooperative collective and personal relationship) with one another—but <u>not</u> to do so in an egoic, separative, world-excluding, xenophobic, and intolerant manner. Rather, My devotees are Called, by Me, to transcend <u>egoity</u> through <u>right</u> and <u>true</u> devotional relationship to Me, <u>and</u> mutually tolerant and peaceful cooperation with one another, <u>and</u> all-tolerating cooperative and compassionate and all-loving and all-including relationship with <u>all</u> of mankind, and with even <u>all</u> beings.

I Give My devotees the "Bright" Force of My own Divine Consciousness Itself, Whereby they can become capable of "Bright" life. I Call for the devotion, but also the intelligently discriminative self-understanding, the rightly and freely living self-discipline, and the full functional capability, of My devotees. I do not Call My devotees to resist or eliminate life, or to strategically escape life, or to identify with the world-excluding ego-centric impulse. I Call My devotees to live a positively functional life. I do not Call My devotees to separate themselves from vital life, from vital enjoyment, from existence in the form of human life. I Call for <u>all</u> the human life-functions to be <u>really</u> and <u>rightly</u> known, and to be <u>really</u> and <u>rightly</u> understood, and to be <u>really</u> and <u>rightly</u> lived (and not reduced by or to the inherently bewildered, and inherently "cultic", or self-centered and fearful, "point of view" of the separate and separative ego-"I"). I Call for <u>every</u> human life-function to be revolved away from self-contraction (or ego-"I"), and (by Means of that revolving turn) to be turned "<u>outwardly</u>" (or expansively, or counter-contractively) to all and All, and (thereby, and always directly, or in an all-and-All-transcending manner) to <u>Me</u>—rather than to be turned merely "<u>inwardly</u>" (or contractively, or counter-expansively), and, as a result, turned away from <u>Me</u> (and from all and All). Thus, I Call for <u>every</u> human life-function to be thoroughly (and life-positively, and in the context of a fully participatory human life) aligned and adapted to <u>Me</u>, and, Thus and Thereby, to be turned and Given to the Realization of Truth (or Reality Itself, Which <u>Is</u> the Only Real God).

Truly benign and positive life-transformations are the characteristic signs of right, true, full, and fully devotional

Satsang with Me, and freely life-positive feeling-energy is the characteristic accompanying "mood" of right, true, full, and fully devotional Satsang with Me. The characteristic life-sign of right, true, full, and fully devotional Satsang with Me is the capability for self-transcending relatedness, based on the free disposition of no-seeking and no-dilemma. Therefore, the characteristic life-sign of right, true, full, and fully devotional Satsang with Me is not the tendency to seek some "other" condition. Rather, the characteristic life-sign of right, true, full, and fully devotional Satsang with Me is freedom from the presumption of dilemma within the <u>present-time</u> condition.

One who rightly, truly, fully, and fully devotionally understands My Words of Divine Self-Revelation and Divine Instruction, and whose life is lived in right, true, full, and fully devotional Satsang with Me, is not necessarily, in function or appearance, "different" from the ordinary (or natural) human being. Such a one has not, necessarily, acquired some special psychic abilities, or visionary abilities, and so on. The "radical" understanding (or root self-understanding) I Give to My devotees is not, itself, the acquisition of <u>any</u> particular "thing" of experience. My any particular devotee may, by reason of his or her developmental tendencies, experience (or precipitate) the arising of extraordinary psycho-physical abilities and extraordinary psycho-physical phenomena, but not <u>necessarily</u>. My every true devotee is simply Awakening (and always Awakened to Me) within the otherwise bewildering "dream" of <u>ordinary</u> <u>human</u> life.

Satsang with Me is a natural (or spontaneously, and not strategically, unfolding) Process, in Which the self-contraction that <u>is</u> each one's suffering is transcended by Means of <u>total</u> psycho-physical (or whole bodily) Communion with My Real (and Really, and tangibly, experienced) Divine (Spiritual, and Transcendental)[16] Presence and Person. My devotee is (as is the case with any and <u>every</u> ego-"I") <u>always</u> <u>tending</u> to be preoccupied with ego-based seeking, but, all the while of his or her life in <u>actively</u> self-surrendering (and really self-forgetting, and, more and more, self-transcending) devotional Communion with Me, I Am <u>Divinely</u> Attracting (and <u>Divinely</u> Acting upon) My true devotee's heart (and total body-mind), and (Thus and Thereby) Dissolving and Vanishing My true devotee's fundamental egoity (and even all of his or her otherwise motivating dilemma and seeking-strategy).

There are <u>two</u> principal tendencies by which I am always being confronted by My devotee. One is the tendency to <u>seek</u>, rather than to truly enjoy and to fully animate the Condition of Satsang with Me. And the other is the tendency to make a self-contracting circle around Me—and, thus, to make a "cult" of ego-"I" (and of the "man in the middle"), or to duplicate the ego-ritual of mere fascination, and of inevitable resistance, and of never-Awakening unconsciousness. Relative to these two tendencies, I Give <u>all</u> My devotees only <u>one</u> resort. It is this true Satsang, the devotionally Me-recognizing, and devotionally to-Me-responding, and always really counter-egoic devotional relationship to <u>Me</u>.

The Great Secret of My own Person, and of My Divine Blessing-Work (now, and forever hereafter), and, therefore, the Great Secret of the only-by-Me Revealed and Given Way of Adidam, Is that I am <u>not</u> the "man in the middle", but I Am Reality Itself, I <u>Am</u> the Only <u>One</u> Who <u>Is</u>, I <u>Am</u> That Which Is Always Already The Case, I <u>Am</u> the Non-Separate (and, necessarily, Divine) Person (or One and Very Self, or One and True Self-Condition) of all and All (<u>Beyond</u> the ego-"I" of every one, and of all, and of All).

Aham Da Asmi. Beloved, I <u>Am</u> Da, the One and Only and Non-Separate and Indivisible Divine Person, the Non-Separate and Indivisible Self-Condition and Source-Condition of all and All. I <u>Am</u> the "Bright" Person, the One and Only and Self-Existing and Self-Radiant Person, Who <u>Is</u> the One and Only and Non-Separate and Indivisible and Indestructible Light of All and all. I Am <u>That</u> One and Only and Non-Separate <u>One</u>. And, <u>As</u> <u>That</u> <u>One</u>, and <u>Only</u> <u>As</u> <u>That</u> <u>One</u>, I Call all human beings to recognize Me, and to respond to Me with right, true, and full devotion (by Means of formal practice of the only-by-Me Revealed and Given Way of Adidam).

I do not tolerate the so-called "cultic" (or ego-made, and ego-reinforcing) approach to Me. I do not tolerate the seeking ego's "cult" of the "man in the middle". I am not a self-deluded ego-man, making much of himself, and looking to include everyone-and-everything around himself for the sake of social and political power. To be the "man in the middle" is to be in a Man-made trap, an absurd mummery of "cultic" devices that enshrines and perpetuates the ego-"I" in one and all. Therefore, I do not make or tolerate the religion-making "cult" of ego-Man. I do not tolerate the inevitable abuses of religion, of Spirituality, of Truth Itself, and of My own Person (even in bodily human Form) that are made (in endless blows and mockeries) by ego-based mankind when the Great Esoteric Truth of devotion to the Adept-Realizer is not rightly understood and rightly practiced.

The Great Means for the Teaching, and the Blessing, and the Awakening, and the Divine Liberating of mankind (and of even all beings) Is the Adept-Realizer Who, by Virtue of True Divine Realization, Is Able to (and, indeed, cannot do otherwise than) Stand In and <u>As</u> the Divine (or Real and Inherent and One and Only) Position, and to <u>Be</u>, Thus and Thereby, the Divine Means (In Person) for the Divine Helping of one and all. This Great Means Is the Great Esoteric Principle of the collective historical Great Tradition[17] of mankind. And Such Adept-Realizers Are (in their Exercise of the Great Esoteric Principle) the Great Revelation-Sources That Are at the Core and Origin of <u>all</u> the right and true religious and Spiritual traditions within the collective historical Great Tradition of mankind.

By Means of My (now, and forever hereafter) Divinely Descended and Divinely "Emerging"[18] Avataric Incarnation, I Am the Ruchira Avatar, Adi Da Samraj—the Divine Heart-Master, the first, the last, and the only Adept-Realizer of the seventh (or Most Perfect, and all-Completing) stage of life.[19] I Am the Ruchira Avatar, Adi Da Samraj, the Avataric Incarnation (and Divine World-Teacher[20]) every-where Promised for the "late-time" (or "dark" epoch)—which "late-time" (or "dark" epoch) is <u>now</u> upon <u>all</u> of mankind. I <u>Am</u> the Great and Only and Non-Separate and (necessarily) Divine Person, Appearing in Man-Form As the Ruchira Avatar, Adi Da Samraj, in order to Teach, and to Bless, and to Awaken, and to Divinely Liberate all of mankind (and even all beings, every "where" in the Cosmic domain). Therefore, by Calling every one and all (and All) to <u>Me</u>, I Call every one and all (and All) <u>Only</u> to the Divine Person, Which <u>Is</u> My own and Very Person (or Very Self, or Very Self-Condition), and Which <u>Is</u> Reality Itself, or Truth Itself, the Indivisible and Indestructible Light That <u>Is</u> the Only Real God, and Which <u>Is</u> the <u>One</u> and <u>Very</u> and <u>Non-Separate</u> and <u>Only</u> Self (or Self-Condition, and Source-Condition) of all and All (Beyond the ego-"I" of every one, and of all, and of All).

The only-by-Me Revealed and Given Way of Adidam necessarily (and As a Unique Divine Gift) requires and involves devotional recognition-response to Me In and Via (and <u>As</u>) My bodily (human) Avataric-Incarnation-Form. However, because I Call every one and all (and All) to Me <u>Only</u> <u>As</u> the Divine Person (or Reality Itself), the only-by-Me Revealed and Given Way of Adidam is not about ego, and egoic seeking, and the egoic (or the so-called "cultic") approach to Me (as the "man in the middle").

According to <u>all</u> the esoteric traditions within the collective historical Great Tradition of mankind, to devotion-ally approach <u>any</u> Adept-Realizer as if he or she is (or is limited to being, or is limited by being) a mere (or "ordinary", or even merely "extraordinary") human entity is the great "sin" (or fault), or the great error whereby the would-be devotee fails to "meet the mark". Indeed, the Single

Greatest Esoteric Teaching common to <u>all</u> the esoteric religious and Spiritual traditions within the collective historical Great Tradition of mankind Is that the Adept-Realizer should <u>always</u> and <u>only</u> (and <u>only</u> devotionally) be recognized and approached <u>As</u> the Embodiment and the Real Presence of <u>That</u> (Reality, or Truth, or Real God) Which would be Realized (Thus and Thereby) by the devotee.

Therefore, <u>no</u> <u>one</u> should misunderstand <u>Me</u>. By Revealing and Confessing My Divine Status to one and all and All, I am not indulging in self-appointment, or in illusions of grandiose Divinity. I am not claiming the "Status" of the "Creator-God" of exoteric (or public, and social, and idealistically pious) religion. Rather, by Standing Firm in the Divine Position (<u>As</u> I <u>Am</u>), and, Thus and Thereby, <u>Refusing</u> to be approached as a mere man, or as a "cult"-figure, or as a "cult"-leader, or to be in any sense defined (and, thereby, trapped, and abused, or mocked) as the "man in the middle", I Am Demonstrating the Most Perfect Fulfillment (and the Most Perfect Integrity, and the Most Perfect Fullness) of the Esoteric, and Most Perfectly <u>Non-Dual</u>, Realization of Reality. And, by Revealing and Giving the Way of Adidam, Which Is the Way of ego-transcending devotion to Me <u>As</u> the One and Only and Non-Separate and (necessarily) Divine Person, I Am (with Most Perfect Integrity, and Most Perfect Fullness) Most Perfectly (and in an all-Completing and all-Unifying Manner) Fulfilling the Primary Esoteric Tradition (and the Great Esoteric Principle) of the collective historical Great Tradition of mankind—Which Primary Esoteric Tradition and Great Esoteric Principle Is the Tradition and the Principle of devotion to the Adept-Realizer <u>As</u> the Very Person and the Direct (or Personal Divine) Helping-Presence of the Eternal and Non-Separate Divine Self-Condition and Source-Condition of all and All.

Whatever (or whoever) is cornered (or trapped on all sides) bites back (and fights, or <u>seeks</u>, to break free). Whatever (or whoever) is "in the middle" (or limited and "centered" by attention) is patterned by (or conformed to) the ego-"I" (and, if objectified as "other", is forced to represent the ego-"I", and is even made a scapegoat for the pains, the sufferings, the powerless ignorance, and the abusive hostility of the ego-"I").

If there is no escape (or no Way out) of the corner (or the "centered" trap) of ego-"I", the heart goes mad, and the body-mind becomes more and more "dark" (bereft of the Divine and Indivisible and Inherently Free Light of Love-Bliss).

I am not the "man in the middle". I do not stand here as a mere man, "middled" to the "center" (or the cornering trap) of ego-based mankind. I am not an ego-"I", or a mere "other", or the representation (and the potential scapegoat) of the ego-"I" of mankind (or of any one at all).

I <u>Am</u> the Indivisible and Non-Separate One, the One and Only and (necessarily) Divine Person—the Perfectly Subjective[21] Self-Condition (and Source-Condition) That Is Perfectly centerless, and Perfectly boundless, Eternally Beyond the "middle" of all and All, and Eternally Surrounding, Pervading, and Blessing all and All.

I <u>Am</u> the Way Beyond the self-cornering (and "other"-cornering) trap of ego-"I".

In this "late-time" (or "dark" epoch) of worldly ego-Man, the collective of mankind is "darkened" (and cornered) by egoity. Therefore, mankind has become mad, Lightless, and, like a cornered "thing", aggressively hostile in its universally competitive fight and bite.

Therefore, I have not Come here merely to stand Manly in the "middle" of mankind, to suffer its biting abuses, or even to be coddled and ignored in a little corner of religious "cultism".

I have Come here to Divinely Liberate one and all (and All) from the "dark" culture and effect of this "late-time", and (now, and forever hereafter) to Divinely Liberate one and all (and All) from the pattern and the act of ego-"I", and (Most Ultimately) to Divinely Translate[22] one and all (and All) Into the Indivisible, Perfectly Subjective, and Eternally Non-Separate Self-Domain of the Divine Love-Bliss-Light.

The ego-"I" is a "centered" (or separate and separative) trap, from which the heart (and even the entire body-mind) must be Retired. I Am the Way (or the Very Means) of that Retirement from egoity. I Refresh the heart (and even the entire body-mind) of My devotee, in every moment My devotee resorts to Me (by devotionally recognizing Me, and devotionally, and ecstatically, and also, often, meditatively, responding to Me) Beyond the "middle", Beyond the "centering" act (or trapping gesture) of ego-"I" (or self-contraction).

I Am the Perfectly Subjective Self-Condition (and Source-Condition) of every one, and of all, and of All—but the Perfectly Subjective Self-Condition (and Source-Condition) is not "within" the ego-"I" (or separate and separative body-mind). The Perfectly Subjective Self-Condition (and Source-Condition) is not in the "center" (or the "middle") of Man (or of mankind). The Perfectly Subjective Self-Condition (and Source-Condition) of one, and of all, and of All Is Inherently centerless, or Always Already Beyond the self-contracted "middle", and to Be Found only "outside" (or by transcending) the bounds of separateness, relatedness, and "difference". Therefore, to Realize the Perfectly Subjective Self-Condition and Source-Condition (or the Perfectly Subjective, and, necessarily, Divine, Heart) of one, and of all, and of All (or even, in any moment, to exceed the ego-trap, and to be Refreshed at heart, and in the total body-mind), it is necessary to feel (and to, ecstatically, and even meditatively, swoon) Beyond the "center" (or Beyond the "point of view" of separate ego-"I" and separative body-mind). Indeed, Most Ultimately, it is only in self-transcendence to the degree of unqualified relatedness (and Most Perfect Divine Samadhi, or Utterly Non-Separate Enstasy) that the Inherently centerless and boundless Divine Self-Condition and Source-

Condition Stands Obvious and Free (and <u>Is</u>, Thus and Thereby, Most Perfectly Realized).

It Is only by Means of Me-recognizing (and to-Me-responding) devotional meditation on Me (and otherwise ecstatic heart-Contemplation of Me), and total, and totally open, and totally self-forgetting psycho-physical Reception of Me, that your madness of heart (and of body-mind) is (now, and now, and now) escaped, and your "darkness" is En-Light-ened (even, at last, Most Perfectly). Therefore, be My true devotee, and, by formally, and rightly, and truly, and fully, and fully devotionally practicing the only-by-Me Revealed and Given Way of Adidam (Which <u>Is</u> the True and Complete Way of the True and Real Divine Heart), always Find Me Beyond your self-"center" in every here and now.

Aham Da Asmi. Beloved, I <u>Am</u> Da. And, because I <u>Am</u> Infinitely and Non-Separately "Bright", all and All <u>Are</u> In My Sphere of "Brightness". By feeling and surrendering Into My Infinite Sphere of Divine Self-"Brightness", My every devotee <u>Is</u> In Me. And, Beyond his or her self-contracting and separative act of ego-"I", My every devotee (self-surrendered Into heart-Communion With Me) <u>Is</u> the One and Only and Non-Separate and Real God I Have Come to Serve, by Means of My Divine Descent, My Divine Avataric Incarnation, and My (now, and forever hereafter) Divine "Emergence" (here, and every "where" in the Cosmic domain).

Notes to
FIRST WORD

1. The ego-"I" is the fundamental self-contraction, or the sense of separate and separative existence.

2. See note 24, p. 160.

3. The Sanskrit phrase "Aham Da Asmi" means "I (Aham) Am (Asmi) Da". The Name "Da", meaning "the One Who Gives", indicates that Avatar Adi Da Samraj is the Supreme Divine Giver, the Avataric Incarnation of the Very Divine Person. (See also note 20, p. 157.)

4. Avatar Adi Da uses "Self-Existing and Self-Radiant" to indicate the two fundamental aspects of the One Divine Person—Existence (or Being, or Consciousness) Itself, and Radiance (or Energy, or Light) Itself.

5. See note 6, pp. 152-53.

6. This passage is Avatar Adi Da's Self-Confession as "Avatar". In Sanskrit, "Ruchira" means "bright, radiant, effulgent". Thus, the Reference "Ruchira Avatar" indicates that Avatar Adi Da Samraj is the "Bright" (or Radiant) Descent of the Divine Reality Itself (or the Divine Truth Itself, Which Is the Only Real God) into the conditional worlds, Appearing here in bodily (human) Form. Avatar Adi Da Samraj is the "Avataric Incarnation", or the Divinely Descended Embodiment, of the Divine Person. The reference "Avataric Incarnation" indicates that Avatar Adi Da Samraj fulfills both the traditional expectation of the East—that the True God-Man is an Avatar, or an utterly Divine "Descent" of Real God in conditionally manifested form—and the traditional expectations of the West—that the True God-Man is an Incarnation, or an utterly human Embodiment of Real God.

7. "The 'late-time', or 'dark' epoch" is a phrase that Avatar Adi Da uses to Describe the present era, in which doubt of God (and of anything at all beyond mortal existence) is more and more pervading the entire world, and in which the separate and separative ego-"I", which is the root of all suffering and conflict, is regarded to be the ultimate principle of life.

8. See note 7, p. 153.

9. The Hindi word "Satsang" literally means "true (or right) relationship", "the company of Truth". In the Way of Adidam, Satsang is the eternal relationship of mutual sacred commitment between Avatar Adi Da Samraj and each true and formally acknowledged practitioner of the Way of Adidam.

10. Avatar Adi Da uses "understanding" to mean "the process of transcending egoity". Thus, to "understand" is to simultaneously observe the activity of the self-contraction and to surrender that activity via devotional resort to Avatar Adi Da Samraj.

Avatar Adi Da has Revealed that, despite their intention to Realize Reality (or Truth, or Real God), all religious and Spiritual traditions (other than the Way of Adidam He has Revealed and Given) are involved, in one manner or another, with the search to satisfy the ego. Only Avatar Adi Da has Revealed the Way to "radically" understand the ego and (in due course, through intensive formal practice of the Way of Adidam, as His formally acknowledged devotee) to most perfectly transcend the ego. Thus, the Way Avatar Adi Da has Given is the "Way of 'Radical' Understanding".

11. The entire practice of the Way of Adidam is founded in heart-recognition of Ruchira Avatar Adi Da Samraj as the Very Divine Being in Person.

AVATAR ADI DA SAMRAJ: The only-by-Me Revealed and Given Way of Adidam (Which is the only-by-Me Revealed and Given Way of the Heart) is the Way of life you live when you rightly, truly, fully, and fully devotionally recognize Me, and when, on that basis, you rightly, truly, fully, and fully devotionally respond to Me.

. . . In responsive devotional recognition of Me, the principal faculties are loosed from the objects to which they are otherwise bound— loosed from the patterns of self-contraction. The faculties turn to Me, and, in that turning, there is tacit recognition of Me, tacit experiential Realization of Me, of Happiness Itself, of My Love-Bliss-Full Condition. That "Locating" of Me opens the body-mind spontaneously. When you have been thus Initiated by Me, it then becomes your responsibility, your sadhana, to continuously Remember Me, to constantly return to this recognition of Me, in which you are Attracted to Me, in which you respond to Me spontaneously with all the principal faculties. ("Recognize My Divine Body and 'Bright' Person, and Let Everything Melt That Is 'Between' You and Me", in *Hridaya Rosary*)

12. See pp. 184-95 for a description of the congregations of Adidam.

13. The Adepts of what Avatar Adi Da calls "the 'Crazy Wisdom' tradition" (of which He is the supreme, seventh stage exemplar) are Realizers of the fourth, fifth, or sixth stages of life in any culture or time who, through spontaneous Free action, blunt Wisdom, and liberating laughter, shock or humor people into self-critical awareness of their egoity, which is a prerequisite for receiving the Realizer's Spiritual Transmission. Typically, such Realizers manifest "Crazy" activity only

occasionally or temporarily, and never for its own sake but only as "skillful means".

Avatar Adi Da Himself has always addressed the ego in a unique "Crazy-Wise" manner, theatrically dramatizing, and poking fun at, the self-contracted habits, predilections, and destinies of His devotees. His "Crazy-Wise" Manner is a Divine Siddhi, an inherent aspect of His Avataric Incarnation. Through His "Crazy-Wise" Speech and Action, Avatar Adi Da Penetrates the being and loosens the patterns of ego-bondage (individually and collectively) in His devotees. The "Shock" of Truth Delivered via His "Crazy Wisdom" humbles and opens the heart, making way for the deeper reception of His Spiritual Blessing.

14. For a description of the Vow and responsibilities associated with the Way of Adidam, see pp. 183-203.

15. "Difference" is the epitome of the egoic presumption of separateness—in contrast with the Realization of Oneness, or Non-"Difference", that is native to Spiritual and Transcendental Divine Self-Consciousness.

16. Avatar Adi Da uses the terms "Spiritual", "Transcendental", and "Divine" in reference to different dimensions of Reality that are Realized progressively in the Way of Adidam. "Spiritual" refers to the reception of the Spirit-Force (in the "basic" and "advanced" contexts of the fourth stage of life and in the context of the fifth stage of life); "Transcendental" refers to the Realization of Consciousness Itself as separate from the world (in the context of the sixth stage of life); and "Divine" refers to the Most Perfect Realization of Consciousness Itself as utterly Non-separate from the world (in the context of the seventh stage of life). (See also note 22, pp. 157-60.)

17. The "Great Tradition" is Avatar Adi Da's term for the total inheritance of human, cultural, religious, magical, mystical, Spiritual, and Transcendental paths, philosophies, and testimonies from all the eras and cultures of humanity, which inheritance has (in the present era of worldwide communication) become the common legacy of mankind. Avatar Adi Da Samraj is the seventh stage, or Divine, Fulfillment of the Great Tradition.

18. On January 11, 1986, Avatar Adi Da passed through a profound Yogic Swoon, which He later Described as the initial Event of His Divine "Emergence". Avatar Adi Da's Divine "Emergence" is an ongoing Process in which His bodily (human) Form has been (and is ever more profoundly and potently being) conformed to Himself, the Very Divine Person, such that His bodily (human) Form is now (and forever

hereafter) an utterly Unobstructed Sign and Agent of His own Divine Being.

19. For Avatar Adi Da's extended Instruction relative to the seven stages of life, see *The Seven Stages Of Life—The Seventeen Companions Of The True Dawn Horse, Book Ten: Transcending The Six Stages Of egoic Life, and Realizing The ego-Transcending Seventh Stage Of Life, In The Divine Way Of Adidam*. (See also note 22, pp. 157-60.)

20. Avatar Adi Da Samraj is the Divine World-Teacher because His Wisdom-Teaching is the uniquely Perfect Instruction to every being—in this (and every) world—in the total process of Divine Enlightenment. Furthermore, Avatar Adi Da Samraj constantly Extends His Regard to the entire world (and the entire Cosmic domain)—not on the political or social level, but as a Spiritual matter, constantly Working to Bless and Purify all beings everywhere.

21. Avatar Adi Da uses "Perfectly Subjective" to Describe the True Divine Source, or "Subject", of the conditional world—as opposed to the conditions, or "objects", of experience. Thus, in the phrase "Perfectly Subjective", the word "Subjective" does not have the sense of "relating to the merely phenomenal experience, or the arbitrary presumptions, of an individual", but, rather, it has the sense of "relating to Consciousness Itself, the True Subject of all apparent experience".

22. In the context of Divine Enlightenment in the seventh stage of life in the Way of Adidam, the Spiritual process continues. Avatar Adi Da has uniquely Revealed the four phases of the seventh stage process: Divine Transfiguration, Divine Transformation, Divine Indifference, and Divine Translation.

Divine Translation is the most ultimate "Event" of the entire process of Divine Awakening. Avatar Adi Da Describes Divine Translation as the Outshining of all noticing of objective conditions, through the infinitely magnified Force of Consciousness Itself. Divine Translation is the Outshining of all destinies, wherein there is no return to the conditional realms.

For Avatar Adi Da's extended Discussion of Divine Translation, see *The All-Completing and Final Divine Revelation To Mankind—The Seventeen Companions Of The True Dawn Horse, Book Eleven: A Summary Description Of The Supreme Yoga Of The Seventh Stage Of Life In The Divine Way Of Adidam*, Part Two, or *The Dawn Horse Testament Of The Ruchira Avatar*, chapter forty-four.

RUCHIRA AVATAR ADI DA SAMRAJ
Adidam Samrajashram (Naitauba), Fiji, 1997

PART ONE

The Search for Truth
Is Absurd and Unnecessary

The Search for Truth
Is Absurd and Unnecessary

I.

AVATAR ADI DA SAMRAJ: It is commonplace for people to say they are "seeking the Truth". It is even regarded as laudable and appropriately modest to Declare that one is only "seeking the Truth".

However, the Way I have Revealed and Given to My devotees, Which is the Way of Adidam[1] (or the Only-by-Me Revealed and Given Way of the Heart), Is the Way of non-seeking. The Way of Adidam Is the Way of No Seeking. Indeed, the consistent practice of non-seeking (or of no-seeking) is the fundamental discipline (or a principal aspect of the fundamental discipline) of the Way of Adidam.

Truth Is That Which Is Always Already The Case. That Which Is Always Already The Case Is (Necessarily) Reality. Therefore, Reality (Itself) Is Truth, and Reality (Itself) Is the Only Truth.

"Consider"[2] the absurdity, the utter immodesty, of suggesting that you are "seeking Reality"!

The Only-by-Me Revealed and Given Way of Adidam is founded on the Assertion of the Finding of Truth, the Assertion of Communion with the Present Reality.

Thus, to practice the Way of Adidam is to Declare the Truth. To practice the Way of Adidam is to practice the life of Truth, not the search for Truth.

To seek Truth is to deny Truth to begin with. To seek Truth is to avoid Truth, constantly.

To seek Reality (Itself) is to deny Reality (Itself). To seek Reality (Itself) is to avoid Reality (Itself), by seeking It.

Notes to the Text of the *Da Love-Ananda Gita* can be found on pp. 151-76.

It is not immodest to Declare the Finding of Truth, because the Real Finding of Truth is, simply, the Finding (or the Acceptance and the Embrace) of Reality Itself.

Rather, to Find (and to Affirm) Truth (or to Accept and to Embrace Reality Itself) is necessary for right life, for true sanity, and for Real Happiness. Indeed, to Find and Affirm Truth, and (Thus) to Accept and Embrace Reality, is necessary for Unqualified Happiness—because Unqualified Happiness Is the Realization of Love-Bliss, and Reality (Itself) Is Love-Bliss. Unqualified (or Self-Existing, Self-Radiant,[3] and Unlimited, or Un-conditional) Love-Bliss Is (Itself) That Which Is Always Already The Case—and Unqualified Love-Bliss (Which Is Happiness Itself) must (having, by Means of Divine Grace, been Found) be constantly Affirmed and Embraced—or else It can never Be Realized.

II.

AVATAR ADI DA SAMRAJ: The *Bhagavad Gita* is one of the principal religious and Spiritual scriptures of the Great (collective) Tradition of mankind.[4] In the *Bhagavad Gita,* the Divine Law is Declared, in the form: "You cannot avoid action. Rather, you have the right—indeed, the obligation—to act. But you do not have a right to the fruits, or the results, of action."

According to this Declaration, you must act. Even the natural patterns of the body-mind and the world make action necessary. But you must renounce the results of every action.

What does this mean? It means that you must purify your motives, such that, eventually, action ceases to be purposed to fulfill desires. Thus, the Divine Law, as It is Declared in the *Bhagavad Gita*, is a kind of prescription for seeking—even a prescription for seeking the state of no-seeking (in which state Truth, Reality, Real God, or Love-Bliss-Happiness is to be Realized). Thus, even all the traditional Declarations of the Divine Law prescribe the action of seeking as the means to, as a <u>result</u>, achieve the state of no-seeking, and, thus, the eventual Realization of Truth, Reality, Real God, or Love-Bliss-Happiness Itself. Indeed, all of the traditions within the Great (collective) Tradition of mankind are prescriptions for seeking Truth, Reality, Real God, or Love-Bliss-Happiness Itself.

The only-by-Me Revealed and Given Way of Adidam is unique. Its uniqueness can be described in many terms, but fundamental to Its uniqueness is the fact that the Way of Adidam is <u>not</u> a way of <u>seeking</u> for Truth, for Reality, for Real God, or for Love-Bliss-Happiness Itself. Rather, the Way of Adidam Is the Way of the always <u>present-time</u> Realization of Truth, Reality, Real God, or Love-Bliss-Happiness Itself.

To practice the Way of Adidam is to have always already Found Truth, Reality, Real God, or Love-Bliss-Happiness Itself. To practice the Way of Adidam is to <u>live</u> Truth, to live <u>in</u> Reality Itself, as a self-surrendering <u>devotee</u> of Reality (or Real God) Itself. Therefore, in Its essence, the Way of Adidam is self-surrender into <u>always</u> <u>present-time</u> (and not merely future-time) Realization of Love-Bliss-Happiness Itself.

In the only-by-Me Revealed and Given Way of Adidam, the Divine Law is (by Me) Declared in terms of Love-Bliss. Love-Bliss <u>Is</u> Reality Itself. If you withdraw from Love-Bliss, or if you withhold yourself from Love-Bliss, or if you deny Love-Bliss, or if you merely <u>seek</u> Love-Bliss—you, inevitably (and by that very <u>act</u>), suffer. As a practitioner of the Way of Adidam, you are My devotee. And, as My devotee, in constant Me-recognizing[5] and to-Me-responding heart-Communion (and total psycho-physical Communion) with Me, you are in constant Communion with <u>Me</u>—the Divine Love-Bliss-Reality. Thus, as My devotee, you always already have the right—and, indeed, the obligation—of Love-Bliss Itself. But your obligation is not merely to <u>seek</u> Love-Bliss. Instead, your always present-time obligation is (by Means of devotional recognition-response to <u>Me</u>) to Realize (and <u>Be</u>) Love-Bliss, and so to animate (or live) Love-Bliss, constantly. You do this not by "inventing" Love-Bliss, not by attempting to self-generate Love-Bliss, but by Realizing <u>Me</u>, in always present-time direct heart-Communion with Me. If you withdraw from Me, you withdraw from Love-Bliss. If you withdraw from My always present-time Divine Self-Revelation (or Divine Self-Manifestation) of Love-Bliss, you suffer. Therefore, do not withdraw from Me, and do not seek Me, but, simply (devotionally), recognize Me, and (by that simple devotional recognition) be devotionally responsive to Me, always Love-Bliss-"Bright",[6] Divinely Self-Revealed before you.

Another aspect of the by-Me-Declared Divine Law can also be noticed in the experience of My devotee: If you <u>cling</u> to any thing or any one, you suffer. To withhold yourself (or to withdraw) from My Divine Presence of Love-Bliss is to suffer the present-time non-Realization of My Condition of Love-Bliss. Likewise, to cling to (or even to anticipate the loss of) any object (or other) in the midst of the act of feeling-participation in My Love-Bliss is, also, to suffer the present-time non-Realization of My Condition of Love-Bliss. My Divine Self-Condition of Inherent Love-Bliss Is egoless (and not contracted) Reality Itself.

The *Bhagavad Gita* Declares that you have the obligation to act, but you have no right to seek or to claim the results, or the fruits, of action. In contrast to this (or, rather, in Most Perfect[7] Fulfillment of it), understand Me in terms of Love-Bliss. I Declare the Divine Law to you in My constant (and always present-time) Self-Revelation of the Divine Love-Bliss to you. Thus, as My responsively devotional (or always ego-surrendering, and ego-forgetting, and ego-transcending) devotee, you have the <u>inherent</u> and <u>constant</u> obligation of Love-Bliss. You have the obligation to <u>Be</u> your Realization of Me, in always present-time heart-Communion with Me, actively, moment to moment. But your participatory (or devotional) <u>manifestation</u> of Me must be egoless, because participatory (or devotional) <u>Realization</u> of Me <u>Is</u>, necessarily, egoless.

It is common "street-religion" to suggest that people should "love" one another, just as it is common "street-religion" to Declare you are "<u>seeking</u> the Truth". But to "love" in the egoic manner is merely to withhold "love" in some instances, and to cling to the object of "love" in other instances. And, in both events (whether withholding or clinging), you (inevitably, and as a direct result of that deficient, or self-contracting, act) suffer.

The ego-"I"[8] is (inherently) characterized by suffering. The self-contraction <u>is</u> suffering. The act of self-contraction <u>is</u> withdrawal from (or contraction away from) the Condition of Love-Bliss. Truth (Found and Declared, rather than merely sought and, thereby, denied) <u>Is</u> the present-time egoless Realization of Love-Bliss (Itself). And the proof of this Realization of Love-Bliss is in your animating (or living) of Love-Bliss (Itself).

To prove your heart-Communion with Me, and your always present-time Realization of My Love-Bliss, your participatory devotional manifestation of My Love-Bliss must be constant—such that you are <u>not</u> withholding love (or withdrawing from, or contracting away from, My Love-Bliss) in any instance, <u>and</u> such that you are <u>not</u> clinging to the other (and, thus and thereby, forgetting Me, and relinquishing self-surrendering devotional participation in My Love-Bliss-Condition) in any instance.

Love, Un-conditionally. Therefore, do not withdraw, or otherwise withhold, love from (or, in any sense or manner, contract from loving) any one at all, or even any thing (or any condition) at all, under any circumstances or conditions at all. Do this <u>Real</u> love by always (in every present-time moment) entering (Un-conditionally) into self-surrendering, self-forgetting, and, always more and more, self-transcending heart-Communion with <u>Me</u> (and always <u>total</u> psycho-physical heart-Communion with <u>My</u>

Love-Bliss-Person)—in the midst of (and via) all relations, and under (and via) all circumstances and conditions.

Love, Un-conditionally. Therefore, do not cling to (or become bondage-bound to) any one at all, or even any thing (or any condition) at all, under any circumstances or conditions at all. Do this Real love by always (in every present-time moment) feeling to and through every one, and every thing, and every circumstance, and every condition—and (from thence) to Me (and, Un-conditionally, into My All-and-all-Surrounding and All-and-all-Pervading Love-Bliss-Person, Beyond every one, and every thing, and every circumstance, and every condition).

This only-by-Me Revealed and Given Divine Law of Real practice of Un-conditional love (not as a form of seeking, or of ego-effort, but as the Really counter-egoic responsive practice of heart-Communion with My Self-Revealed and Self-Transmitted Divine Love-Bliss-Person) Is the Inherently Perfect Basis for your always present-time Realization of Me, and for your (Thus) always present-time devotional Realization and devotional manifestation of Divine Love-Bliss-Happiness. Therefore, this only-by-Me Self-Revealed Divine Law of Real practice of Un-conditional love Describes the constant obligation of all My rightly, truly, fully, and fully devotionally practicing devotees.

My true devotees do not seek Me, and they do not deny Me. Their Embrace of Me is egoless. Their "Bonding"[9] to Me is (inherently) non-egoic, and constantly counter-egoic—and, therefore, It is not binding.

All ordinary "bonding" is, characteristically, ego-based—it is about clinging to a conditional "other" (and, thereby, forgetting Me). As My true devotee, your "Bonding"-Embrace of Me is unique, because of your devotional recognition of Me, and your self-surrendering (and self-forgetting, and, more and more, self-transcending) devotional response to Me. It is not ego-based "bonding", to the degree of bondage. It is devotional "Bonding" to Me, to the Degree of No-bondage.

Your devotional heart-Communion with Me purifies all relations in which you are animated, but It tests you profoundly. Your heart-Communion with Me tests you in your tendency to withhold yourself (or contract) from the Condition of Love-Bliss Itself, and It tests you in your tendency to cling to what is egoically "loved".

You like to congratulate yourself, or feel good, about loving the ones you love, but it is serving you to do so— because you would not have them disappear or die. You would have your love of them (and their love of you) be constant (or never interrupted) and (thus) "forever"—but that cannot (as such) be so.

To cling to an other is (inevitably, and always presently) to suffer the merely temporary nature of all merely conditional existence (of both "self" and "other"). Nevertheless, to withhold (or withdraw, or contract) from an other is, likewise (inevitably, and always presently), to suffer the non-Realization of Love-Bliss-Happiness in the context of the present-time pattern of the conditions of merely conditional existence. Therefore, your always present-time devotional Communion with Me must be freely and fully manifested in all relations. You must never withhold love (or withdraw from, or contract away from, My Love-Bliss), and you must never cling to the other (and, thus and thereby, forget Me, and relinquish self-surrendering devotional participation in My Love-Bliss-Condition).

Mine Is the Fullest (and all-Completing) Declaration of the Divine Law: My devotee is not here to seek Me, but, in every present-time moment, to Commune with Me, and (Thus, devotionally, egolessly, and Non-separately) to Realize Me. Therefore, My devotee must always manifest Me in the responsively self-transcending manner—not by dissociation, and not by clinging-bondage, but by unqualified relatedness—by selfless, or directly ego-transcending, relatedness.

My Divine Self-Revelation and My Divine Law (or Way) Are the Great Secret of transcending egoic fear, sorrow, and anger. This Is the Great Secret of how to be free in relationships of apparent "bonding". This Is the Great Secret of how to live, such that life is not about bondage.

The only-by-Me Revealed and Given Way of Adidam is not the way of seeking. It is not the way of self-contracted withholding (or of ascetical, or otherwise fearful, sorrowful, or angry, dissociation). It is also not the way of self-indulgent ego-bondage (or of self-indulgence itself, fearfully, sorrowfully, or angrily seeking others, or things, or conditions, and fearfully, sorrowfully, or angrily clinging to others, or things, or conditions). Rather, the only-by-Me Revealed and Given Way of Adidam Is the Way of constant (and constantly egoless) Love-Bliss-Communion with Me.

Love-Bliss-Communion with Me is the Great Secret of transcending your bondage to all others and all things and all conditions. Nevertheless, Love-Bliss-Communion with Me is not a matter of withholding yourself from all others and all things and all conditions. Love-Bliss-Communion with Me is not about strategically dissociating from the gross[10] physical body and its world of relations. Love-Bliss-Communion with Me is not about seeking to dissociate from the gross physical body or to leave this world. Love-Bliss-Communion with Me is not about seeking to be rid of <u>any</u> one or <u>any</u> thing or <u>any</u> condition.

Love-Bliss-Communion with Me is not about leaving any present relation in order to seek or find a "better" other! Thus, for example, My devotee should persistently regard his or her any present intimate partner, once chosen and confirmed in My Company, as his or her intimate partner according to the by Me Self-Revealed Divine Law (and, therefore, not as one who can be casually set aside, or, otherwise, relinquished without most profoundly self-testing personal and cultural "consideration").

As My devotee, you should not regard your any present intimate partner to be there merely to fulfill <u>your</u> inclinations, such that you would leave him or her when you are frustrated in those inclinations. Persistently Accept your any present intimate partner, and all your loved ones, and all your friends, and even all My devotees as My Instruments—effectively there to serve My Purpose of bringing to an end all of your egoic impulse and suffering. Therefore, if your any present intimate partner frustrates you, this is very, very good! Such frustration clearly serves My Purpose—perhaps not your purpose (as the ego-"I"), but My Divine (and inherently egoless, and always counter-egoic) Purpose! This is how your (otherwise) egoic "bondings" become means for transcending ego-bondage—not by dissociating from them, but by living them in Communion with Me, and going through the ego-transcending Ordeal that all relations require of you in the devotional practice of Love-Bliss-Communion with Me.

The mass of things and conditions and beings is present now. You like some of it, and you dislike some of it. This is the character of the ego-"I"—the character (or conditional "persona") who does not Know the Truth. That un-Knowing character withholds in some cases and clings in other cases. That, altogether and constantly, is exactly and always what the ego-"I" does.

My Declaration of the Divine Law is Stated in terms of Divine Love-Bliss (and of humanly activated love). Therefore, as My true devotee, you are not merely obliged to act (while having no right to the "fruits" of your action—whatever that may mean to you), but, rather, you are obliged to love (never withholding yourself from My Love-Bliss, and, likewise, never forgetting My Love-Bliss by self-contracted clinging to any other, or any thing, or any condition).

You cannot be free of your clinging to any other by dissociating from him or her, but only by entering into Love-Bliss-Communion with Me—so profoundly that you transcend your self-contraction (both as your motive of withdrawal and your motive of clinging).

In Communion with My Love-Bliss-Person, you have the obligation (and the urge, and the heart-capability) to love, under all circumstances, and in all relations. You have no right to (in any instance) withhold yourself from love, and you have no right to (in any instance) cling to any object of love. This is the Paradox of Truth, of Reality Itself, of Real God, of Self-Existing, Self-Radiant, Divine-"Bright" Consciousness Itself, Which Is Love-Bliss Itself, Me-Present.

My true devotee does not seek Me. My true devotee Declares Me, loves Me, Affirms that I Am. Your proper modesty is not in Declaring that you are seeking the Truth, but in Declaring and living the Finding of Truth, in Declaring and living the inherent Love-Bliss-Fullness of the One Who Is Always Already The Case. This is what it is to be a true man or woman, rather than a seeker (or an ego, separate and separative). You, as My devotee, must (by your manner and signs of living, and by your very mind, and your every word) constantly Affirm and Declare your Finding of Truth—not in the "gleeful" (or merely "cultic") manner, but as My true devotee, who allows himself or herself to be tested by the Divine Law and Person of Love-Bliss Itself. Therefore, My devotee is not called by Me to animate mere "social" love, but to responsively manifest the Divine Love-Bliss Itself—My Own Person, Found and (in constantly present-time Communion) Realized in self-forgetting, and manifested in non-withholding and non-clinging.

For My devotee, non-clinging is not a matter of somehow dissociating from this or that one, or from this or that thing or condition that you might, otherwise, cling to. It is not that at all. Rather, for My devotee, non-clinging is a matter of manifesting My Love-Bliss, simply as the Radiance (Self-Revealed by Me) in his or her heart-Communion with Me, and living the Ordeal of tested ego-surrender to the (At Last) Most Perfect Degree, Such That his or her actively manifested Realization of My Love-Bliss goes (always more and more profoundly) Beyond all of death and change and ending, Beyond all egoic fear, sorrow, and anger, Beyond all withholding and all clinging.

Therefore, in the only-by-Me Revealed and Given Way of Adidam, My true devotee does not seek to leave this world, or to leave the gross physical body, or to reduce the gross physical body to a nothing of strategically achieved emptiness and desirelessness (or motionlessness). Rather, in the only-by-Me Revealed and Given Way of Adidam, the present-time world and the present-time body are <u>always</u> Accepted—utterly, wholeheartedly, in <u>Me</u>.

III.

AVATAR ADI DA SAMRAJ: Spiritual Teachers, in their various degrees of Real-God-Realization, have often suggested that, having thus so Realized Real God, they have Agreed to Enter into the human body, perhaps only as far down as the eyes, or, perhaps, the throat, or, at most, the heart. Ramakrishna, for example, used to suggest this. However, I, in My Avataric Incarnation[11] here, have Agreed to Accept (and to Embrace) the even gross physical conditions of the gross physical body, down to the toes, including all that comes, inevitably, with that "unamusing" situation. I have Done this in order to Most Perfectly (and Most Fully, and Truly Completely, and, Really Finally) Demonstrate My Own Divine Person here—in order to Self-Manifest (or Demonstrate) My Divine Self <u>Utterly</u>, without the slightest withholding, and Radiant to the Degree that Exceeds all mere clinging, by Embracing all conditional relations in an "Heroic"[12] Spiritual Act of Self-Demonstrated Divine Love-Bliss—even, Thereby, passing through the "dark" time[13] of mortality, passing through the confrontation with change and necessary natural endings, in the case of This (My Avataric-Incarnation-Body), and in the case of Its relations, which include all and All. In order to Perform My Divine "Emergence"[14] here (and every "where" in the Cosmic domain), I have had to Accept all relations, Absolutely, without the slightest withholding, and without mere clinging. This is the unique Nature of My Leela,[15] My Divine Leela of Avataric Incarnation here.

In the Incident in Which My Divine "Emergence" was Initiated, on January 11, 1986, I Told you that I had Descended to the toes, that I had Embraced this limited condition Absolutely. I Asked those around Me at the time to observe the Divine "Sorrow" in My Face, which "Sorrow" is Absolute, and which "Sorrow" My (from then, and forever thereafter) Divine "Emergence" Work here (and every "where" in the Cosmic domain) is "Brightly" (now, and forever hereafter) Overcoming, in all cases—not by Me dissociating from My Profound "Sorrow" of Descent, but by My constant Acceptance of the "Sorrow" (or Feeling-Depth of Sympathetic Love) inherent in all My conditionally appearing and disappearing relations. I am not Speaking to you as an "Abstracted" (or Separate and Separative) "Other", dissociating from here, coming down only partially into the body. I am not Proud of asceticism. I am not Looking Forward to "Leaving". I am not Dwelling "Elsewhere".

Always, in My (now, and forever hereafter) Divine "Emergence" Work, I Am, Dwelling here, and every "where" in the Cosmic domain, moment by moment—constantly Dissolving a "Sorrow" more Immense than you can contemplate or imagine. The Overcoming of universal egoic sorrow, and fear, and anger—the Overcoming (in and as every one, and all, and All) of the imposition of apparent "difference",[16] of mortality, of change—Is the Radiant "Bright" Nature of My Divine "Emergence" Work. Now, and forever hereafter, My Divine "Emergence" Work (Divinely Liberating all and All) Goes On here, and every "where" in the Cosmic domain.

The Divine Translation[17] of all and All into My Divine Self-Domain[18] Is the Most Ultimate Fulfillment of My Divine "Emergence" Work. Therefore, This Work cannot be Finally Demonstrated (in the case of every one, and all, and All) within the physical Lifetime of This (My Avataric-Incarnation-Body) here. My Divine "Emergence" Work is My Forever Work.

I am not seeking anything whatsoever. I Am Utterly Entered into this apparent psycho-physical confinement, this seeming entrapment of All-and-all-Multiplied body-minds and worlds. Therefore, I Am Suffering all of this, Completely (even in My Own bodily human Form), without the slightest ability to be distracted from it. This is the Nature of My intentional Embrace of all and All.

My "Bright" Outshining of all egoic fear, sorrow, and anger is the Divine Translation of all beings. The suffering of egoic fear, sorrow, and anger will not end (for every one, and all, and All) until there is the Divine Translation of all beings, all worlds, all conditions. And yet—uniquely, paradoxically, and all the while of My (now, and forever hereafter) Divine "Emergence" Work—there is not the slightest egoic fear, sorrow, or anger in Me.

Enter most fully into most profound heart-Communion with Me, and you will understand What I Am Saying.

My Own Love-Bliss Is My Divine Means (and the Only Really and Truly Effective Means) in this vast Cosmic domain of egoic fear, sorrow, and anger. The Effective (or Real) Dissolution of your egoic fear, sorrow, and anger is in your Me-"Bright" devotional manifestation of My Love-Bliss, under all the conditions that would, otherwise, be egoically fearful, sorrowful, or angering. Therefore, in the only-by-Me Revealed and Given Way of Adidam, you are tested according to My Divine Law of Love-Bliss Itself, in your every moment of heart-Communion with Me.

There is always (in every conditionally manifested body-mind) the tendency to withhold (or withdraw) and the tendency to cling. These are the fundamental signs of ego-"I" (or self-contraction).

In true (or total psycho-physical) heart-Communion with Me (self-surrendering, self-forgetting, and, more and more, self-transcending), you transcend both withholding and clinging.

This is how you are "Brightened" by Me.

This is the Nature of My "Bright" Kiln[19] of Adidam.

The Way of practice I have Revealed and Given is not the search for Truth, not the search for Reality, not the search for Real God, not the search for Love-Bliss-Happiness—not the search for Me. Rather, the Way of practice I have Revealed and Given Is the Way and the practice of always present-time Love-Communion with Me—Such That, in every moment, you are "Brightened" by Me, "Brightened" by My Love-Bliss (and, necessarily, in every moment, going through the testing Ordeal of transcending your every tendency to withhold or to cling).

If you understand what I have just now Told you, then you understand the uniqueness of Adidam.

IV.

AVATAR ADI DA SAMRAJ: Only the ego-"I" would say that it is seeking for Truth. Only the ego-"I" can seek for Truth—because Truth is the one thing that the ego-"I" has not.

Only the ego-"I" could Declare that it is seeking for Reality Itself. Only the ego-"I" would suggest that it is laudable to seek for Truth, or for Reality Itself. And, indeed, mankind has, in fact, made an entire culture (and even many cultures) on the basis of egoic seeking.

The right understanding and Really effective transcending of this fault is the process by which human civilization can be made right—because human civilization will not (and cannot) ever be made right by seeker's religion or seeker's science or seeker's anything.

All kinds of things may come to be known, but the Truth (or the, necessarily, Divine Reality, Itself) must be constantly Affirmed, from the beginning, or the Truth (or Reality Itself) can never (Itself) be Known. Ordinary religion and ordinary science are means for seeking and gaining experience, for seeking and gaining a kind of conditional knowledge, even a kind of control (or power) over experience. But the ways of seeking are not about Finding the Truth.

It is impossible to seek the Truth and, as a result of the seeking of It, Find It.

It is impossible to seek Reality Itself, and, as a result of the seeking of It, Find It.

Therefore, you must transcend the search itself.

The only-by-Me Revealed and Given Way of Adidam Is the One and Only (and, altogether, Divinely Self-Revealed) Way (and Real practice) of understanding and transcending the search for Truth, the search for Reality Itself, the search for Real God, the search for Happiness (or Divine Love-Bliss) Itself, and, indeed, all seeking—by directly (and constantly) transcending "search" (and the egoic cause of seeking) itself.

The only-by-Me Revealed and Given Way of Adidam is not a way, or means, for seeking Truth, or Reality, or Real God, or Happiness—or for achieving Truth, or Reality, or Real God, or Happiness as a result of that search.

The only-by-Me Revealed and Given Way of Adidam is the Way (and, therefore, the active, and, necessarily, ego-transcending practice) of the always present-time devotional (or Me-recognizing, and to-Me-responding) Realization of Love-Bliss, Which Is Happiness, Truth, Reality, and the only Real God.

RUCHIRA AVATAR ADI DA SAMRAJ
Adidam Samrajashram (Naitauba), Fiji, 1997

PART TWO

Da Love-Ananda Gita
(The Free Gift Of The Divine Love-Bliss)

1.

The (Ultimate) Nature of the world (and how it is arising) is inherently (and tacitly) obvious, if you <u>remain</u> in a state of pleasurable oneness with whatever and all that presently arises.

2.

To remain in a state of pleasurable oneness with whatever and all that presently arises, you must (necessarily, and always presently) Realize inherently Love-Blissful Unity with whatever and all that presently arises.

3.

Inherently Love-Blissful Unity with whatever and all that presently arises is (Itself, or inherently) non-separation (or no-contraction) from whatever and all that presently arises.

4.

Separation (or contraction) from the world (or whatever and all that is presently arising) is (unfortunately) precisely the first and constant (and inherently problematic) thing done by <u>all</u> those who make efforts to find out (or to account for) how the world is arising (and What Is its Ultimate Nature).

5.

Separation (or self-contraction) is the first (and foundation) gesture made by anyone who has a problem, or who is seeking, or who is making an effort to account for anything whatsoever.

6.

Pleasurable oneness (or inherently Love-Blissful Unity) is inherent (or necessarily and priorly the case, no matter what conditions do or do not arise), and, therefore, pleasurable oneness (or inherently Love-Blissful Unity) is (necessarily) uncaused, and Real (or always already the case, and always already in, of, and Identical to Truth), whereas separateness (or "Difference") is always conditional, conditionally caused (or only conditionally apparent), and illusory (or always already dissociated from Reality and Truth).

7.

Pleasurable oneness (or inherently Love-Blissful Unity) need not (and cannot fruitfully) be sought.

8.

Pleasurable oneness (or inherently Love-Blissful Unity) can be (apparently) lost, by the <u>act</u> of self-contraction (and, thereby, of apparent separation, separateness, and separativeness).

9.

Pleasure-seeking, Love-Bliss-seeking, or Unity-seeking efforts (of any kind) are <u>only</u> parts of a strategic (and always already un-Happy) adventure, and such effort and adventure are entered into <u>only</u> by those who are already (presently) separating (or contracting) themselves in (and from) What <u>Is</u>, and such adventurers are seeking <u>only</u> because they are already, presently, separating (or contracting) themselves in (and from) What <u>Is</u>.

10.

Therefore, it is necessary to understand this (or self-contraction itself), and (by the transcending of self-contraction itself) to Recover Awareness of the obvious (or inherent) Love-Bliss-Unity (and, Thus, to inherently account for <u>everything</u>, and also, Thereby, to solve, or inherently transcend, <u>all</u> problems).

11.

This understanding (and this Recovery) cannot (fruitfully) be sought, for all seeking is inherently associated with an already present act of self-contraction (and, thereby, of separation, separateness, and separativeness).

12.

True understanding is itself inherent, or always already, or Native to even (apparently) conditional existence itself.

13.

Therefore, if such understanding is not already Realized in the present, it must (and can only) be Realized by Divine Grace (as a Free Gift).

14.

Aham Da Asmi.[20] I **Am** Da (the Divine Giver), the Person and the Means of this Divine Grace.

15.

I **Am** Love-Ananda[21] (the Divine Love-Bliss), the Presence and the Way of this Free Gift.

16.

The understanding of which I Speak is (if Most Perfectly Realized) the Most Perfectly Ultimate (or seventh stage[22]) Capability to (inherently) Divinely Recognize[23] whatever arises.

17.

Most Perfect understanding is the Capability to directly (immediately) transcend dilemma, all problems, and all seeking.

18.

$\mathbb{M}$ost Perfect understanding is the Capability to "radically"[24] (always already) transcend self-contraction (and all of separation, separateness, and separativeness).

19.

$\mathbb{M}$ost Perfect understanding is the Capability inherent in Love-Bliss Itself (Which <u>Is</u> the Heart Itself).

20.

$\mathbb{M}$ost Perfect understanding is the Capability inherent in the always already, or most prior, Unity (with Which the Heart Itself, As Love-Bliss Itself, Is inherently One).

21.

$\mathbb{I}$ have, by Means of the Submission, Work, and Word of My here-Speaking Revelation-Body, thoroughly Revealed and Described the Great (and Complete) Process Wherein and Whereby the Heart Itself (or Love-Bliss-Unity Itself) is (Ultimately) Most Perfectly Realized.

22.

$\mathbb{T}$hat Great (and Complete) Process (Which Is the only-by-Me Revealed and Given Way of Adidam, or the only-by-Me Revealed and Given Way of the Heart) is Described (in every detail and elaboration) in My summary (Written, and forever Speaking) Word of Heart (in many Works).[25]

23.

$\mathbb{T}$hat summary Word is True, and that Great Process Is indeed the Process (elaborate in Its totality of details) Wherein the Inherently Perfect Tacit Obviousness (of non-separateness, of no-seeking, of no-contraction, and of Love-Ananda, My Love-Bliss Itself) is (progressively, and, yet, always directly and presently[26]) Realized.

24.

The Principle (or Great Means) of that Great Process Is Itself an Extreme Simplicity (as simple to describe as that Great Process is Itself necessarily complex in Its total description).

25.

Ruchira Avatara Bhakti Yoga[27] (to which I, sometimes, refer, descriptively, by means of the general term "Ishta-Guru Bhakti Yoga"[28]), which Yoga is the responsive (or Me-Recognizing, and to-Me-responding) and constant counter-egoic, and even total psycho-physical, effort of self-surrendering, self-forgetting, and, more and more (and, Ultimately, Most Perfectly), self-transcending devotion to Me and devotional Communion with Me (the Ruchira Avatar, the Da Avatar, the Hridaya Avatar, the Love-Ananda Avatar, the Avabhasa Avatar, the Santosha Avatar,[29] the Realizer, the Revealer, and the Very Revelation of the Real and True and One and Only Divine Person, the One and Only Self-Condition and Source-Condition of all and All, the One and Only Self of all and All, Who Is, or Which Is, Da, the Heart Itself, the "Bright" Itself, and Love-Bliss Itself), and which Yoga is the moment to moment fulfillment of My Great Admonition to all My devotees, to always Invoke Me, feel Me, breathe Me, and serve Me (and this constantly exercised via the surrender, the forgetting, and the transcending of the self-contracted body, and self-contracted emotion, or all of self-contracted, and reactive, and, altogether, limited, feeling, and self-contracted mind, even at its root, which is attention itself, and even every self-contracted breath, and, altogether, even all of separate and separative self, in moment to moment, and truly, or unlimitedly, heart-felt, and whole bodily receptive, and fully breathing, and only-by-Me Distracted devotional Contemplation of My bodily human Form, My Spiritual, and Always Blessing, Presence, and My Very, and Inherently Perfect, State[30]), Is the Great (and only-by-My-Grace Given) Means Wherein and Whereby the Great Process of the only-by-Me Revealed and Given Way of Adidam is Accomplished, and the Great (and only-by-My-Grace Given) Means of Ruchira Avatara Bhakti Yoga is practiced in its fullest right form by all (necessarily, formal) practitioners of the only-by-Me Revealed and Given Way of Adidam who, as the sign of their devotional response to Me, formally embrace, and consistently demonstrate, the right, true, full, and fully devotional practice (and all aspects of the practice) of the only-by-Me Revealed and Given Way of Adidam, and who do so in full accordance with My *Hridaya Rosary*,[31] and who are, thus (and necessarily), formally practicing members of either the first congregation or the second congregation[32] of My formally practicing devotees, and who are, as such, always currently, or in always then present-time, formally approved by the Ruchira Sannyasin Order of the Tantric Renunciates of Adidam[33] to engage this fullest right form of Ruchira Avatara Bhakti Yoga, as My true devotees who rightly, and truly, and truly devotionally Recognize Me as the Only One Who Is (and Who must be Recognized, and Realized, by each and every one of all, and by all and All), and who really and truly Recognize (or Know) Me, by, truly and deeply, heart-receiving, and heart-understanding, and (in this root-devotional sense) heart-hearing My own Me-Revealing Words of Divine Self-Confession of Who I Am, and by, truly and deeply, heart-enjoying and heart-praising My own Me-Revealing Acts, or Leelas, of Divine Self-Revelation of Who I Am, and by constantly, and truly, and deeply heart-Invoking Me, and by, thus and thereby, always exercising their heart-feeling toward Me and to Me (beyond the ego-"I" and beyond the body-mind), and, in this constant feeling-Invocation, really (and, only and entirely, by My own Me-Revealing Grace) heart-Finding and heart-Receiving Me, and who, in this

Great Manner, inherently and immediately Recognize Me (and, in this root-devotional sense, heart-see Me), as I Divinely <u>Am</u>, the One and Only and Inherently "Bright" Person, the Divine Heart-Master of All and all, the "Bright" Itself, Self-Existing, Self-Radiant, and Self-Revealed, in Person, Tangibly, Undoubtably, Utterly Converting the heart and the mind and the breath and the body from ego-"I" (or the "Act of Narcissus",[34] which is self-contraction) to the Ecstatic "Bhava"[35] of only-Me-Beholding Love-Bliss-Happiness.

26.

For all those who would (either formally or informally) study the only-by-Me Revealed and Given Way of Adidam, My summary (Written, and forever Speaking) Word of Heart (in many Works) is (now, and forever hereafter) Given (by Me) for their hearts and minds to comprehend.

27.

For all those who would (necessarily, formally) practice the only-by-Me Revealed and Given Way of Adidam, My summary (Written, and forever Speaking) Word of Heart (in many Works) is (now, and forever hereafter) Given (by Me) for their formal (and formally guided, and formally accountable) application (within any of the four congregations of My devotees[36]).

28.

And for all those who would, by (necessarily, formally) practicing the only-by-Me Revealed and Given Way of Adidam, surrender and forget themselves in the Divine and Inherently Perfect Truth (of non-separateness, of no-seeking, of no-contraction, and of Love-Ananda, My Love-Bliss Itself), I am always (now, and forever hereafter) here for their devotional Contemplation (within any of the four congregations of My devotees).

29.

Realization of the Most Ultimate (or seventh stage) Wisdom-Unity, Truth-Obviousness, and (Divine) Recognition-Capability (through the truly most intensive and profound practice of the fullest right form of Ruchira Avatara Bhakti Yoga, necessarily in the context of either the first congregation or the second congregation of formal approach to Me) is a matter of My Giving Grace and My Graceful Self-Revelation.

30.

My bodily (human) Form (Which has, by Virtue of My Spiritual, and, here, very human, Ordeal of Heart-"Bright" Descent Into the Cosmic Domain, Become Most Perfectly Conformed to Me, to Love-Ananda, to the Divine Love-Bliss Itself) Is (Itself) the Teaching (and the Always First Realizer of Its Truth).

31.

My Spiritual (and Always Blessing) Presence (Which Is My "Bright" Heart-Transmission of Love-Ananda, the Divine Love-Bliss Itself) Is the (Always Me-Revealing) Means.

32.

My Very (and Inherently Perfect) State (Which Is Love-Ananda, the Divine Love-Bliss Itself) Is the (necessarily, Divine) Revelation Itself.

33.

Therefore, devotional Contemplation of My bodily (human) Form, and (via My bodily human Form) My Spiritual (and Always Blessing) Presence, and (via My Spiritual, and Always Blessing, Presence) My Very (and Inherently Perfect) State, even, Most Ultimately, to the degree of Perfect Oneness with Me (and Perfect no-contraction and non-separation from all and All, transcending all seeking and all of egoity itself, by Means

of devotional surrender and heart-conformity to Me, to
Love-Ananda, to the Divine Love-Bliss Itself) Is the Heart-
Way That I Offer to you and to all.

34.

I Say to you: First and always, in your bodily (human)
form, be the always Me-Recognizing, and responsively
(and actively) Me-serving, devotee of My bodily (human)
Form, and (as your devotion, your service, your self-
discipline, and your self-understanding mature, or,
eventually, become matured, by that responsively, and
actively, self-surrendering, and self-forgetting, and, more
and more, self-purifying and self-contraction-transcending
feeling-Contemplation of Me) you will (by Means of My
Giving Grace and My Graceful Self-Revelation) also
become heart-sensitive (and, altogether, psycho-physically
sensitive) to My "Bright" and True, and Always Blessing,
Spiritual Presence (Which Is Love-Bliss Itself), and (as an
always Me-Recognizing, and responsively, and actively,
Me-serving devotee of My bodily human Form, and
always, Thereby, becoming more and more Deeply
sensitive to My Spiritual, and Always Blessing, Presence)
you will (by Means of My Giving Grace and My Graceful
Self-Revelation) sometimes also (in the Always Deepening
Revelation of My Ceaselessly Heart-Transmitted Love-Bliss)
spontaneously Intuit and Contemplate the beginningless,
endless, centerless, non-separate, and boundless Deep of
My Very (and Inherently Perfect) State.

35.

Therefore, simply (Merely, and intentionally, but on
the basis of a fundamental, and fundamentally effortless,
or Freely responsive, heart-Recognition of Me and
feeling-Attraction to Me) Contemplate My bodily (human)
Form, My Spiritual (and Always Blessing) Presence, and
My Very (and Inherently Perfect) State, and do this
Contemplation progressively (as My Giving Grace and My

Graceful Self-Revelation Determine the progress), such
that (more and more) you allow My bodily (human)
Form to <u>Attract</u> (and <u>Keep</u>) your (truly feeling) attention,
and This such that (more and more) you allow My
Spiritual (and Always Blessing) Presence to <u>Pervade</u> your
body-mind, and This such that (more and more) you
allow My Very (and Inherently Perfect) State to Abide
(in Person) in your (by Means of My Giving Grace and
My Graceful Self-Revelation) egoless (or Only-Me-
Contemplating) heart.

36.

Simply (Merely), by <u>feeling</u> (and even, randomly
and occasionally, by Name[37]), Remember and Invoke (or
otherwise directly Regard) My bodily (human) Form,[38]
and (Merely by <u>feeling</u>) Contemplate (and Meditate on)
My bodily (human) Form, and (by <u>feeling</u> Me, Thus)
progressively <u>feel</u> My Spiritual (and Always Blessing)
Presence, the "Bright" Giving-Force Heart-Radiated (by
Me, and As Me) in, and via, and around, and everywhere
beyond, and Perfectly prior to, My bodily (human) Form,
and (by <u>feeling</u> My Spiritual, and Always Blessing,
Presence, Thus) be progressively Yielded to My Very (and
Inherently Perfect) State, until (Thereby, in any moment)
your own act of self-contraction (and, thus, of separation,
separateness, and separativeness) is dissolved, released,
vanished, or forgotten in Me.

37.

Do this <u>feeling</u>-Contemplation (progressively, as My
Giving Grace and My Graceful Self-Revelation will have
it) at random (daily), and more and more constantly, and
(in accordance with your formal congregation of formal
approach to Me) as a developing formal Meditation,[39] and,
Thus, by always keeping attention on Me, be purified
and released of the casual distractions (and the
sometimes and self-enclosed sleep) of attention.

38.

Realize the Obvious Truth (of non-separateness, of no-seeking, of no-contraction, and of Love-Ananda, My Love-Bliss Itself), Thus, by My Grace Alone, again and again.

39.

Therefore, Contemplate Me, Meditate on Me, actively (responsively) Yield the motions of body, breath, emotion, and mind to Me (and into the Heart of My bodily human Form, My Spiritual, and Always Blessing, Presence, and My Very, and Inherently Perfect, State), such that, by Means of My Giving Grace and My Graceful Self-Revelation, you Realize true heart-Communion with Me, and (Thus and Thereby) become self-surrendered into the Obvious Truth (of non-separateness, of no-seeking, of no-contraction, and of Love-Ananda, My Love-Bliss Itself), Revealed (by My Grace) to be Inherent in pleasurable (psycho-physically self-surrendered) oneness with whatever and all that presently arises, and, more and more, exercise the Thus by Me Given Capability for transcending all problems and all seeking, or all apparent limitations on love, and on My Gracefully Transmitted Love-Bliss Itself, if they arise, and when they arise.

40.

The only-by-Me Revealed and Given Way of Adidam (Which is the only-by-Me Revealed and Given Way of the Heart) is the "radical" (or most direct) Way of the Heart Itself, Which (Itself) "radically" (or most directly) Realizes (and, Ultimately, Is) the inherent (or Native, or always already, and necessarily Divine) Truth.

41.

The only-by-Me Revealed and Given Way of Adidam (Which is the only-by-Me Revealed and Given Way of the Heart) is the Way of non-separateness, or the Heart-Way of counter-active (or actively self-transcending) responsibility for the (otherwise <u>always</u> arising) action that is egoity (the ego, the ego-"I", or the primal "Act of Narcissus", which is the act of self-contraction, and the constant action of separation, separateness, and separativeness).

42.

The only-by-Me Revealed and Given Way of Adidam (Which is the only-by-Me Revealed and Given Way of the Heart) is the devotional Way of Me-Recognizing heart-responsive self-submission to (and into) My Form and Presence and State of Grace, Which is the devotional Way of (more and more effective) counter-egoic action, the Way of active (and more and more effective) devotional surrender of self-contraction, and the devotionally active Way of (more and more effective) self-transcendence, through self-surrendering, self-forgetting, and self-transcending heart-Communion with (and psycho-physical Infusion by) the (by My Grace) Self-Revealed, Inherently Non-separate, Inherently Perfect, Perfectly Subjective,[40] and Inherently "Bright" (or Self-Existing and Self-Radiant) Reality and Truth.

43.

The only-by-Me Revealed and Given Way of Adidam (Which is the only-by-Me Revealed and Given Way of the Heart) is the Way of Divine Grace, Wherein the Free Gift of "radical" self-understanding is Given to all and Awakened in all, in the moment (or in any moment) of self-transcending Recognition and responsive feeling-Contemplation of My bodily (human) Form, My Spiritual (and Always Blessing) Presence, and My Very (and Inherently Perfect) State.

44.

Therefore, if you are responding to This (My Word of Heart), and if you are (by This) heart-Moved to transcend and Be Free of the otherwise constant "Act (and Results) of Narcissus", and if you are heart-Attracted to (or toward) My bodily (human) Form (because It Is Heart-"Bright"), and to (or toward) My Spiritual (and Always Blessing) Presence (because It Is the Free Transmission of Love-Bliss), and to (or toward) My Very (and Inherently Perfect) State (because It Self-Reveals the Truth), and if you would (by always Merely Remembering and Contemplating Me) forget your separate and separative self (the ego-"I", or self-contraction, appearing as body, emotion, and all of mind) in Me, then Yield to Me, embrace My Seven Giving Gifts,[41] and practice the Divine Way of Adidam in My Gracefully Self-Revealing Company.

45.

The only-by-Me Revealed and Given Way of Adidam is the (necessarily, formal) <u>practice</u> of Ruchira Avatara Satsang,[42] or the self-surrendering, and self-forgetting, and (really, effectively) self-purifying and self-contraction-transcending <u>work</u> of constant, Me-Recognizing, devotionally heart-responsive, and effectively counter-egoic (or intentionally and effectively self-Yielding and self-forgetting) <u>feeling</u>-Contemplation of My bodily (human) Form, My Spiritual (and Always Blessing) Presence, and My Very (and Inherently Perfect) State.

46.

Therefore, by always first (responsively, actively, and intentionally) "Locating" the <u>feeling</u>-Place in you that already and presently and effortlessly feels Attracted to My bodily (human) Form, and My Spiritual (and Always Blessing) Presence, and My Very (and Inherently Perfect) State, Yield (responsively, actively, and intentionally) to the <u>feeling</u> of the Inherent "Bright" Attractiveness of My bodily (human) Form, and Yield (responsively, actively, and intentionally) to the <u>feeling</u> of the Inherent "Bright" Attractiveness of My Spiritual (and Always Blessing, and progressively Revealed) Presence, and, by all of this, responsively, actively, and intentionally Yield (and more and more deeply forget) your ego-"I" (or your own action of separation, separateness, and separativeness) in the "Bright" and Very Space of My (progressively) Revealed (and Inherently Perfect) State.

47.

You (necessarily) become (or conform to the likeness of) whatever you Contemplate, or Meditate on, or even think about.

48.

Therefore, Contemplate Me, and transcend even all thought by Meditating on Me.

49.

Do not Meditate on your separate self (your states, your experiences, your presumed knowledge, your dilemma, your problem, or your search), and do not perpetuate self-contraction (by strategies of independent effort, and by adventures of either self-glorification or self-destruction, within or without), but (always, immediately) transcend self-Meditation, personal states, conditional experiences, presumptions of knowledge, and all of dilemma, problem, and search (Merely by Remembering Me, and Invoking Me, and Recognizing Me, and Meditating on Me, and, Therefore, Merely by surrendering to <u>Me</u>, not by self-concerned effort, or by isolated and concerned manipulation of conditions themselves, but by simply, and intentionally, and more and more deeply, responding and Yielding to the always presently Available feeling of the Inherent "Bright"

Attractiveness of My bodily human Form, and of My Spiritual, and Always Blessing, Presence, and of My Very, and Inherently Perfect, State), and (Thus, by Means of the always presently Available Grace That Is My Good Company) always and actively feel beyond and (really, effectively) transcend your separate and separative self (Merely by feeling, and Thereby Contemplating, Me).

50.

Do this Contemplation for Its own Sake, and not passively and partially (as if <u>waiting</u> for devotion to happen <u>to</u> you, rather than always presently Remembering, Invoking, and Recognizing Me, and, Thereupon, responsively <u>allowing</u> the presently inevitable feeling of My Inherent "Bright" Attractiveness, and, Thereby, most simply, <u>always</u> and <u>fully</u> <u>activating</u> My always Given and Giving Gift of devotion), and not cleverly and strategically (with all effort and no response, intent but not Yielding, stressful with the <u>seeking</u> of Me, rather than Happy with the <u>Finding</u> of Me), but do this Contemplation constantly, always, Merely, and by heart, and (Thus) by feeling <u>to</u> My bodily (human) Form, and by feeling <u>into</u> My Spiritual (and Always Blessing) Presence, and, more and more, by feeling My Very and Freely Revealed and Freely (Inherently) Perfect State.

51.

Therefore, actively (responsively) <u>be</u> My devotee, Recognizing Me (or heart-Knowing <u>Who</u> I Truly, Really, and, necessarily, Divinely <u>Am</u>), and the Obvious Truth (of non-separateness, of no-seeking, of no-contraction, and of Love-Ananda, My Love-Bliss Itself) will (Freely) be Given to you, by Me, in every moment, and (to the degree you make Room for Me in the Place of your feeling, by surrendering thought, and even every form of self-contraction, in self-forgetting Me-Remembrance) the Obvious Truth (of non-separateness, of no-seeking, of no-contraction, and of Love-Ananda, My Love-Bliss Itself) will (Thus and Thereby) be Found and Received by you (as My Giving Grace and My Graceful Self-Revelation will have it, in any moment).

52.

Now, and forever hereafter, this Simplicity is the essential practice (and the essence of the entire practice of the only-by-Me Revealed and Given Way of Adidam) to which I Call every one.

53.

All those who would so (and, necessarily, formally) practice are Called by Me to embrace, and (according to My Instructions, as Given for application within each one's formal congregation of formal approach to Me) to progressively develop, the original (or most basic) functional, practical, and relational disciplines (and the original, or most basic, cultural obligations)[43] I have Described (and Given) in and by My summary (Written, and forever Speaking) Word of Heart (in many Works).

54.

Those disciplines and practices are the (most basic) necessary evidence of the Me-Recognizing devotional response to Me.

55.

Those disciplines and practices should be responsively and positively embraced (and, by real, and, necessarily, formal, practice, thoroughly "considered" and developed) in the context of the essential practice of the only-by-Me Revealed and Given Way of Adidam, which essential practice is (according to the requirements of My devotee's formal congregation of formal approach to Me) daily (formal, and, otherwise, random, and more and more constant), and always (responsively, actively, intentionally) body-opening-yielding, and deeply feeling (and reactive-emotion-forgetting), and really mind-forgetting, and altogether and truly self-contraction-forgetting, feeling-Contemplation of My bodily (human) Form, My Spiritual (and Always Blessing) Presence, and My Very (and Inherently Perfect) State.

56.

When their signs of responsive Recognition of Me (and of Growth in the only-by-Me Revealed and Given Way of Adidam) Allow, My devotees are Given Access to My Blessing-Seat, and each one should (insofar as it is practically possible) come to Me[44] (at the Place, or Places, of My Blessing-Seat appropriate for his or her Access to Me, in accordance with his or her formal congregation of formal approach to Me, and, as the case may be, with his or her form and stage of practice[45] of the only-by-Me Revealed and Given Way of Adidam), and this as often as their right and true and truly Growing practice of the only-by-Me Revealed and Given Way of Adidam, and their present, and, altogether, consistently demonstrated, signs of real and true heart-Recognition of Me and heart-Resort to Me, Allow (and truly Require).

57.

During the (physical) Lifetime of My bodily (human) Form (here), I may Freely Manifest My Seclusions, Offerings, and Blessing-Wanderings any where, but I will always (forever), during and after (and forever after) the (physical) Lifetime of My bodily (human) Form (here), be Really Present at Adidam Samrajashram (the Island of Naitauba in Fiji, Which Island is, now, and forever hereafter, My Great Hermitage, Where I have Established My Self Spiritually in "Brightest" Perpetuity)[46] for the Sake of all and All.

58.

During the (physical) Lifetime of My bodily (human) Form (here), I may Freely Manifest My Seclusions, Offerings, and Blessing-Wanderings any where, but I will always (forever), during and after (and forever after) the (physical) Lifetime of My bodily (human) Form (here), be Really Present at The Mountain Of Attention (in northern California) and Love-Ananda Mahal (in Kauai, Hawaii),[47] the two Sanctuaries I have Directly Empowered and Established for constant Pilgrimages and Retreats (and every other truly Me-Invoking, and Me-Recognizing, and Me-Serving Sacred use) by the formal congregations of My devotees (and to be thus used according to the Principles, Rules, and Instructions Given by Me to the Ruchira Sannyasin Order of the Tantric Renunciates of Adidam, which formal Order of Tantric Renunciates has been, and is, now, and forever hereafter, formally Appointed by Me to be the culturally governing Authority relative to My Great Island-Hermitage, and My Directly-by-Me Empowered Pilgrimage and Retreat Sanctuaries, and all four of the formal congregations of My formally practicing devotees, during, and forever after, the physical Lifetime of My bodily human Form here).

59.

At all times, and in all places, daily and always, all My (necessarily, formally practicing) devotees should (constantly) Contemplate My bodily (human) Form, My Spiritual (and Always Blessing) Presence, and My Very (and Inherently Perfect) State, and (as required, and as permitted, in accordance with each one's formal congregation, and, as the case may be, form, and formal stage, of formal approach to Me) they should do this at My Great Island-Hermitage, and at the Directly-by-Me Empowered Pilgrimage and Retreat Sanctuaries, and, otherwise (always, day to day, as required, or, otherwise, allowed, by each one's formal congregation and circumstance of formal approach to Me), within the formal communities[48] of My devotees (who are formally acknowledged as such by the formally appointed representatives of the sacred cultural and congregational gathering formally Established by Me, and by the Ruchira Sannyasin Order of the Tantric Renunciates of Adidam, the culturally governing Authority formally Established by Me), and they should do this (always) even under all the other and ordinary circumstances of every day, for I will always (forever), during and after (and forever after) the (physical) Lifetime of My bodily (human) Form (here), be Really Present even every then and there (and, therefore, every where and when) for all My (necessarily, formally practicing) devotees.

60.

I am here only for this Satsang (of My devotees, Recognizing Me, and heart-surrendering to Me, to enjoy the "Bright"-Blessed Ordeal of totally psycho-physically enacted self-surrendering, self-forgetting, and self-transcending feeling-Communion with Me, the One and Only and Very Person to be Realized by each and all and All).

61.

I no longer Teach (or Submit to seem in the ordinary likeness of every one and all, in order to Reflect them to themselves, and, Thus and Thereby, to Prove the necessity of ego-transcendence, and, altogether, in order to Reveal and Describe the Great Means and the Great Process of the Heart-Way of non-separateness), but, now, and forever hereafter, during and after (and forever after) the (physical) Lifetime of My bodily (human) Form (here), having already Fully and Completely Done My First (or Teaching) Work (and such that It will Live and Work forever, through My summary Written, and forever Speaking, Word of Heart in many Works, and through the recorded, remembered, and constantly retold Leelas of all of My Teaching Life and Work, and through the recorded, and forever Living, Images of My bodily human Sign), I only Call each one and all to true and constant, and truly Me-Recognizing, devotional Contemplation of Me, As Only I Appear and Function here, and, truly, As I Am, in order that, now, and forever hereafter, during and after (and forever after) the (physical) Lifetime of My bodily (human) Form (here), I may Do My Great, or Divinely "Emerging", Blessing Work with every one and all and All.

62.

Therefore, now, and forever hereafter, during and after (and forever after) the (physical) Lifetime of My bodily (human) Form (here), I, for the Sake of their true and constant devotional Contemplation of Me, Am "Bright" to Give (or Spiritually Awaken in, and Require of) all My devotees the Gift of constant devotional Recognition and devotional love of Me, because true and constant devotional Contemplation of Me is (and, in every moment, requires) truly responsive (and, therefore, truly Me-Recognizing, and really self-surrendering, self-forgetting, and self-transcending) heart-Resort to Me.

63.

Likewise, now, and forever hereafter, during and after (and forever after) the (physical) Lifetime of My bodily (human) Form (here), I, for the Sake of their true and constant devotional Contemplation of Me, Am "Bright" to Give (or Spiritually Awaken in, and Require of) all My devotees the Gift of constant devotional service to Me, because true and constant devotional Contemplation of Me is (and, in every functional, practical, or relational context or circumstance, requires) truly responsive (and, therefore, truly Me-Recognizing, and really self-surrendering, self-forgetting, and self-transcending) heart-attention to Me.

64.

And, now, and forever hereafter, during and after (and forever after) the (physical) Lifetime of My bodily (human) Form (here), I, for the Sake of their true and constant devotional Contemplation of Me, Am "Bright" to Give (or Spiritually Awaken in, and Require of) all My devotees the Gift of constant (and, altogether, devotionally inspired) self-discipline, because true and constant devotional Contemplation of Me is (and, in every context or circumstance, requires) truly responsive (and, therefore, truly Me-Recognizing, and really self-surrendering, self-forgetting, and self-transcending) heart-obedience and heart-conformity to Me.

65.

Now, and forever hereafter, during and after (and forever after) the (physical) Lifetime of My bodily (human) Form (here), I am <u>here</u>, "Bright" <u>As</u> I <u>Am</u>.

66.

I am here (now, and forever hereafter) for Only One Purpose: to Bless and Awaken those who Recognize Me, Resort to Me, and Contemplate Me.

67.

My summary (Written, and forever Speaking) Word of Heart relative to the Extreme Simplicity That Is the Great Means of the only-by-Me Revealed and Given Way of Adidam, and relative to the progressive process of necessary (or, otherwise, potential) developmental stages[49] (and the technically more "elaborate" practices, as well as the technically "simpler" practices, and the technically "simplest" practices[50]) of the only-by-Me Revealed and Given Way of Adidam, is, now, and forever hereafter, during and after (and forever after) the (physical) Lifetime of My bodily (human) Form (here), Fully and Finally and Completely Given here, and My summary (Written, and

forever Speaking) Word of Heart is, now, and forever
hereafter, during and after (and forever after) the
(physical) Lifetime of My bodily (human) Form (here),
to be openly and everywhere Communicated here (as I
have Written It in Its Full, Final, and Complete Forms),
so that everyone (as every one) may read My summary
(Written, and forever Speaking) Word and (by personal
response, as and whenever they will) become My
devotees, and so that all My devotees may (by self-testing
study) "consider" My summary (Written, and forever
Speaking) Word and (by progressive application) develop
their practice (in accordance with each one's formal
congregation of formal approach to Me and, as the case
may be, with each one's eventually proven choice of
Manner, course, and form of the practice) of the only-
by-Me Revealed and Given Way of Adidam.

68.

Those of My devotees (in the second congregation
of formal approach to Me) who, in due course, by Means
of My Giving Grace and My Graceful Self-Revelation,
stably demonstrate the (original) maturing signs of the
only-by-Me Revealed and Given Way of Adidam, and
who, necessarily, formally embrace the right, true, full,
and fully devotional practice of the only-by-Me Revealed
and Given Way of Adidam, and who do so in full
accordance with My *Hridaya Rosary* (with always current,
or always then present-time, formal approval by the
Ruchira Sannyasin Order of the Tantric Renunciates
of Adidam), may (if they choose, and if they qualify)
enter (formally) into the technically "fully elaborated"
(or "elaborately detailed") course of the only-by-Me
Revealed and Given Way of Adidam (which technically
"fully elaborated", or "elaborately detailed", course is,
necessarily, and only, engaged by formal members of
the first congregation of formal approach to Me).

69.

Those of My devotees who choose (and qualify) to practice the technically "fully elaborated" form of the only-by-Me Revealed and Given Way of Adidam must do so under continuous and formal guidance within (and by) one or the other of the (formal) renunciate orders[51] originally established (and formally appointed) by Me for the Sake of all My (thus formally and technically "elaborately") practicing devotees, and they must allow their practice and their discipline to be (thus and thereby) formally measured and determined by technically "elaborately detailed" stages.

70.

Those of My devotees who enter the technically "fully elaborated" course of the only-by-Me Revealed and Given Way of Adidam must (formally, progressively, and as necessary) enter into (and develop) all the by Me Given disciplines, practices, stages, and Realizations of the technically "fully elaborated" form of the only-by-Me Revealed and Given Way of Adidam, and they must do so in a (formally, progressively, and personally appropriate) renunciate Manner.

71.

However, most (necessarily, formal) practitioners of the only-by-Me Revealed and Given Way of Adidam will not choose (and qualify) to embrace the (necessarily, formal renunciate) practice required in the technically "fully elaborated" course of the only-by-Me Revealed and Given Way of Adidam, but they will, indeed, choose (and qualify for) the practice of either the technically "simplest" form of the only-by-Me Revealed and Given Way of Adidam (as formal members of either the second or the third or the fourth congregation of formal approach to Me) or the technically "simpler" form of the only-by-Me Revealed and Given Way of Adidam (necessarily, as formal members of the second congregation of formal approach to Me), and, therefore (in that either "simpler" or "simplest" Manner), they will love Me, and they will Contemplate Me, and (by "simpler", or "simplest", but always true and fullest self-surrendering, self-forgetting, and, more and more, self-transcending devotion to Me) they will always heart-Reside with Me.

72.

The practice and the discipline of My devotees who (as formal members of either the second, the third, or the fourth congregation of formal approach to Me) choose (and qualify) to (necessarily, formally) practice the technically "simplest" form of the only-by-Me Revealed and Given Way of Adidam, and the practice and the discipline of My devotees who (necessarily, as formal members of the second congregation of formal approach to Me) choose (and qualify) to (necessarily, formally) practice the technically "simpler" form of the only-by-Me Revealed and Given Way of Adidam, should not be practiced, measured, or determined according to the fullest (or formal renunciate, and technically "fully elaborated") formal descriptions and measures (or according to the most intensive expectations) of the technically "fully elaborated" form of the only-by-Me Revealed and Given Way of Adidam, but their practice must, nonetheless, be engaged both seriously and consistently, and their practice must necessarily be formally and consistently monitored and measured relative to the progressive development of the (primary) developmental Signs of devotional Recognition of Me, and of responsive (and truly self-surrendering and self-forgetting) devotion to Me, and truly self-surrendering and self-forgetting service to Me, and (as required, according to My Instructions, as Given for application within their formal congregation of formal approach to Me) really self-observing and self-purifying (functional, practical, relational, and cultural) self-discipline, embraced in truly self-surrendering and self-forgetting response to Me, and truly self-surrendering and self-forgetting, and always self-testing, study-"consideration" of My Word, and increasingly meditative, and more and more profoundly self-surrendering and self-forgetting, feeling-Contemplation of Me, and they must formally (and rightly) maintain (and cultivate) their participation in (and their practice-accountability to) the sacred cultural gathering established (and formally appointed) by Me for the Sake of all formal practitioners (and all formal congregations) of the only-by-Me Revealed and Given Way of Adidam, and they must do all of this persistently (and always in and by Means of devotional Contemplation of My bodily human Form, My Spiritual, and Always Blessing, Presence, and My Very, and Inherently Perfect, State), no matter how profound the Process of Reception of Me (or, otherwise, no matter how advanced, or even Ultimate,[52] the Process or the Event of Realization of Me) may become, or (otherwise) seem to be.

73.

In any case, the basic (or essential) practice for all who (necessarily, formally) practice the only-by-Me Revealed and Given Way of Adidam is (in its inherent Simplicity) just that of Me-Recognizing (and responsive, and responsible) feeling-Contemplation of My bodily (human) Form, My Spiritual (and Always Blessing) Presence, and My Very (and Inherently Perfect) State.

74.

Therefore, I Embrace all (necessarily, formal) practitioners of the only-by-Me Revealed and Given Way of Adidam, and I Embrace each one and all of them Simply (Merely) as My devotees (who are all Merely Contemplating Me).

75.

$\mathbb{M}$y Blessing of My devotees always Transmits the Same Gift to each and all, for I always Give, and Freely Give, the One and Only and Divine Gift of My "Bright" Self-Revelation to each and all.

76.

$\mathbb{M}$y Blessing of My devotees is <u>always</u> Full of My "Bright" Spirit-Power, Given for the Sake of the Heart-Awakening of every one and all of My devotees.

77.

$\mathbb{B}$ecause My Blessing-Gift is always only the Divine Gift of My "Bright" Self-Revelation, there are not different kinds of Blessings Given by Me for each kind and (as the case may be) developmental stage of practice of the only-by-Me Revealed and Given Way of Adidam, but there are different modes, forms, kinds, stages, and degrees of devotional approach to Me and of devotional Access to Me (according to which formal congregation of formal approach to Me is formally chosen by My devotee, and for which he or she is, then currently, or in the then present-time, truly qualified).

78.

$\mathbb{B}$ecause of My always constant, Giving, Full, and Perfect Blessing Grace, and because My Blessing-Gift is always the Divine Gift of My "Bright" Self-Revelation, it is possible for any one to practice the only-by-Me Revealed and Given Way of Adidam (in one or the other of the four formal congregations of formal approach to Me), and that practice potentially (and more and more readily and profoundly) Realizes (by Means of My Giving Grace and My Graceful Self-Revelation) pleasurable oneness (or inherently Love-Blissful Unity) with whatever and all that presently arises, if any one will (necessarily, formally) practice at least the technically "simplest" form of the only-by-Me Revealed and Given Way of Adidam, and if any one will (Thereby, actively) respond to Me (with truly Me-Recognizing, and really Me-Contemplating, and, altogether, effectively self-transcending devotion, and in constant and self-transcending service), and if any one will (Thereby, responsively and consistently, according to My Instructions, as Given for application within his or her formal congregation of formal approach to Me) embrace true (functional, practical, relational, and cultural) self-discipline in My Company, and if any one will (progressively) allow every kind of (Thus Inspired and Accomplished) change and release of body, emotion, mind, and separate self.

79.

Indeed, not even any other form of the Conscious Process[53] (or the Process of devotion to Me that specifically controls, or surrenders and transcends, the egoic, or self-contracting, gesture and tendency of attention) need necessarily (or, otherwise, constantly or regularly) be practiced in order to Receive My Giving Grace and My Graceful Self-Revelation, if only My devotee will (regularly, randomly, and more and more constantly) surrender self-contraction (Merely by Means of Me-Remembering, and Me-Invoking, and Me-Recognizing, and truly heart-responsive, and really self-surrendering, self-forgetting, and more and more effectively self-transcending feeling-Contemplation of My bodily human Form, My Spiritual, and Always Blessing, Presence, and My Very, and Inherently Perfect, State), and not even any more intensive (or, otherwise, technically more "elaborate") form of Conductivity[54] (or the whole bodily, physical, emotional, and mental, "conscious exercise" of breath, bodily energy, and, potentially, My Spirit-Force) need necessarily be practiced in order to Receive My Giving Grace and My Graceful Self-Revelation, if only My devotee will (entirely and

Merely by Means of Me-Remembering, and Me-Invoking, and Me-Recognizing, and truly heart-responsive, and really self-surrendering, self-forgetting, and more and more effectively self-transcending feeling-Contemplation of My bodily human Form, My Spiritual, and Always Blessing, Presence, and My Very, and Inherently Perfect, State) embrace and maintain (and, on that basis, develop), according to My Instructions, as Given for application within his or her formal congregation of formal approach to Me, basic functional, practical, relational, and cultural, and, altogether, self-purifying, self-discipline (including the most basic "conscious exercise" of breath and bodily energy, which, in the case of My devotees in the first and second congregations of formal approach to Me, is, in due course, by Means of My Giving Grace and My Graceful Self-Revelation, spontaneously Converted into truly devotional, or heart-responsive, Reception and Conductivity of My "Bright" Transmitted Spiritual, and Always Blessing, Presence).

80.

If only My devotee will (truly devotionally, and rightly, and, necessarily, formally) practice at least the technically "simplest" form of the only-by-Me Revealed and Given Way of Adidam, the Obvious Truth (of non-separateness, of no-seeking, of no-contraction, and of Love-Ananda, My Love-Bliss Itself) will, by Means of My Giving Grace and My Graceful Self-Revelation, be (in random moments, and, potentially, more and more readily and profoundly) Revealed (and Found, and Received) as the Obvious.

81.

In the course of that Process of Revelation (and Finding, and Receiving), many insights and experiences and responsibilities may arise.

82.

In any case (no matter what arises), it is only
necessary to maintain (and, otherwise, progressively to
develop or intensify) right and true functional, practical,
relational, cultural, and, altogether, self-responsible self-
discipline (according to My Instructions, as Given by Me
for application by My formally practicing devotees,
according to each one's formal congregation, and, as the
case may be, form, and formal stage, of formal approach
to Me), and, on that basis, to rightly and truly practice
(according to My Instructions, as Given by Me for
application by My formally practicing devotees, according
to each one's formal congregation, and, as the case may
be, form, and formal stage, of formal approach to Me) at
least technically "simplest" (and regular, and also random,
and more and more constant, and truly, deeply self-
surrendering, self-forgetting, and effectively self-
transcending) devotional (and Me-serving) Contemplation
of My bodily (human) Form, My Spiritual (and Always
Blessing) Presence, and My Very (and Inherently Perfect)
State.

83.

The Most Ultimate and Most Perfect (or true, and
only-by-Me Revealed and Given, seventh stage)
Realization and Capability is the Real Potential <u>only</u> of
<u>My</u> (necessarily, formally practicing) devotees, and,
necessarily (because of all that is required for That
Realization and Capability), <u>only</u> of those of My devotees
who formally embrace the right, true, full, and fully
devotional practice of the only-by-Me Revealed and
Given Way of Adidam (as formal, and truly most
intensively and profoundly practicing, members of the
first congregation of formal approach to Me, or,
otherwise, as formal, and progressively intensively and
profoundly practicing, and, at least eventually, truly most
intensively and profoundly practicing, members of the

second congregation of formal approach to Me), and
who consistently (and truly devotionally) Recognize Me
and Resort to Me, either (in the context of the first
congregation of formal approach to Me) in the technically
"fully elaborated" Manner (and by a progressively more
technical development of practice in the spontaneously
developing context of the however may be necessary
advanced and Ultimate stages of life in the only-by-Me
Revealed and Given Way of Adidam) or (in the context
of the second congregation of formal approach to Me)
in the technically "simpler" (or even "simplest") Manner
(and by the maintenance of a consistently "simpler",
or even "simplest", technical responsibility, in the
spontaneously developing context of the however may
be necessary advanced and Ultimate stages of life in the
only-by-Me Revealed and Given Way of Adidam), and
who practice the only-by-Me Revealed and Given Way of
Adidam in full accordance with My *Hridaya Rosary*
(with always current, or always then present-time, formal
approval by the Ruchira Sannyasin Order of the Tantric
Renunciates of Adidam), and, indeed, even the only-by-
Me Given Great Graces of True Hearing and True Seeing[55]
(as Described, by Me, in My summary Written, and
forever Speaking, Word of Heart) are the Real Potential
<u>only</u> of such (necessarily, formally practicing) devotees
of Mine, who, as members of either the first congregation
or the second congregation of formal approach to Me,
formally embrace the right, true, full, and fully devotional
practice of the only-by-Me Revealed and Given Way of
Adidam, and who do so in full accordance with My
Hridaya Rosary, with always current, or always then
present-time, formal approval by the Ruchira Sannyasin
Order of the Tantric Renunciates of Adidam (whereas
My formally practicing devotees within the third and the
fourth congregations of formal approach to Me practice,
and are, by Me, Given the practice of, <u>only</u> a rudimentary
form of the beginner's Listening[56] practice of devotion to

Me, with only the lesser potential of insights, and experiences, and responsibilities that rudimentary practice makes possible, and <u>Not</u> the Real Potential of True Hearing and True Seeing, and Most Perfect Me-Realization, unless, at least eventually, such devotees of Mine choose to embrace the complete, Fully-To-Me Listening, and, Really Potentially, Truly Me-Hearing, Truly Me-Seeing, and Most Perfectly Me-Realizing practice of the only-by-Me Revealed and Given Way of Adidam, within, at least, the second congregation of formal approach to Me, and, perhaps, eventually, the first congregation of formal approach to Me), but even <u>any</u> and <u>every</u> formal devotee of <u>Mine</u> (in any of the four formal congregations of formal approach to Me) is fully Instructed by Me and (if he or she consistently, and truly devotionally, Resorts to Me) constantly Blessed by Me (at heart, and in his or her total body-mind) to (potentially, in random moments, and, as may be the case, more and more readily and profoundly—if he or she will practice the only-by-Me Revealed and Given Way of Adidam according to My Instructions Given for his or her formal congregation, and, as the case may be, form, and formal stage, of formal approach to Me) Find and Receive Me, and (Thus and Thereby—in the manner, and to the degree, that is possible, according to his or her formal congregation, and, as the case may be, form, and formal stage, of formal approach to Me) to be self-surrendered into the Obvious Truth (of non-separateness, of no-seeking, of no-contraction, and of Love-Ananda, My Love-Bliss Itself) That Is, by Means of My Giving Grace and My Graceful Self-Revelation, Realized to Be Inherent in any and every moment of pleasurable oneness (or inherently Love-Blissful Unity) with whatever and all that presently arises.

84.

In any and every moment of devotional Contemplation of My bodily (human) Form, My Spiritual (and Always Blessing) Presence, and My Very (and Inherently Perfect) State, each one will, by Means of My Giving Grace and My Graceful Self-Revelation, Find and Receive Me according to the quality and strength of his or her Me-Recognizing and truly responsive (and effectively self-surrendering, self-forgetting, and self-transcending) devotion to Me.

85.

In any and every moment of devotional Contemplation of My bodily (human) Form, My Spiritual (and Always Blessing) Presence, and My Very (and Inherently Perfect) State, each one will, by Means of My Giving Grace and My Graceful Self-Revelation, Find and Receive Me according to the presence or absence of the various kinds of egoic limitations that characterize and enforce a physical, psycho-physical, or (otherwise) merely psychic (or mind-made) point of view.

86.

In any and every moment of devotional Contemplation of My bodily (human) Form, My Spiritual (and Always Blessing) Presence, and My Very (and Inherently Perfect) State, each one will, by Means of My Giving Grace and My Graceful Self-Revelation, Find and Receive Me according to his or her relative (and effective) willingness to be released from the present point of view (and, Most Ultimately, in the case of My devotees in the first and second congregations of formal approach to Me who Most Perfectly Realize Me, even from every possible point of view, or all the egoic stages of life).

87.

Each and every one of My devotees (in each and all of the four formal congregations of formal approach to Me) is Called by Me to enter the advanced and the Ultimate stages of life and practice in the Way of Adidam (by, at least eventually, choosing to become, and, in due course, qualifying and practicing as, a formal, and formally fully accountable, member of either the first congregation or the second congregation of formal approach to Me), and (thus, thereby, and in due course) to Receive (and, potentially, to Realize) the inherent Heart-Capability to Stand Free (and to Demonstrate the seventh, and inherently Most Perfect, and truly Most Ultimate, stage of life), and this Capability and Freedom is to be Received (and, Most Ultimately, Realized) by Means of My Giving Grace and My Graceful Self-Revelation (and as My Giving Grace and My Graceful Self-Revelation will have it), and Only (Merely) through truly Me-Recognizing, heart-responsive, and really self-surrendering, self-forgetting, and self-transcending devotional Contemplation of My bodily (human) Form, My Spiritual (and Always Blessing) Presence, and My Very (and Inherently Perfect) State.

88.

Therefore, Listen to Me and Hear Me: You have already eaten the meal of separateness.

89.

Now you must relinquish that awful meal (and Be, purified of separate and separative self).

90.

You do not Require (and you should not seek) any "thing" from Me (to add to your already separate and deluded self).

91.

I Am (My Self) What you Require, and I am here to Require every "thing" of you.

92.

You must relinquish (or surrender) your ego-"I" (your experience, your presumed knowledge, your separateness, all your forms of egoic "bonding", and even all your "things", within and without) to Find and Realize the Fullness That Is Me.

93.

Therefore, Come to Me to Realize Me, and do not run from Me after tasting the meal of knowledge and experience (like a dog runs from its master with a bone).

94.

Having Come to Me, do not look within your body or your mind to discover whether you have received some "thing" from Me (to satisfy your little pouch of separateness).

95.

Rather, surrender and release your separate (or self-contracted, self-contracting, separative, and always seeking) self (including your entire body, your breath, your emotions, your mind, your knowledge, and all your experiences) by Means of the Me-Recognizing, heart-responsive, and, thus, responsively, self-surrendering, self-forgetting, and self-transcending feeling-Contemplation of Me (including All of My bodily human Form, My Spiritual, and Always Blessing, Presence, and My Very, and Inherently Perfect, State), and (Thus and Thereby) Grow to Luxuriate in My Love-Bliss-Presence.

96.

If (by active feeling-Contemplation) you surrender and release your separate self to Me, then not any meal of "things" (or effects), but <u>Only</u> I (My bodily human Form, My Spiritual, and Always Blessing, Presence, and My Very, and Inherently Perfect, State) Am the Gift, the Object, the State, and the Realization.

97.

Therefore, Come to Me, and for <u>Me</u> Only, "Bond" to Me, and to <u>Me</u> Only, and Stay with Me, and with <u>Me</u> Only (forever), and you will (by This) Realize <u>Me</u>, truly, really, and Only.

98.

I <u>Am</u> Da Love-Ananda, the Giver and the Free Gift, Who <u>Is</u> Love-Bliss Itself, the Truth and the Reality Given, and Revealed, and Found, and Received (and, Ultimately, Most Perfectly Realized), by Means of My Blessing Grace, when egoity (or the ego-"I" of self-contraction) is surrendered, forgotten, and transcended in responsive (Me-Recognizing, and total psycho-physical) feeling-Contemplation of My bodily (human) Form, My Spiritual (and Always Blessing) Presence, and My Very (and Inherently Perfect) State, to the degree of non-separateness, no-seeking, and no-contraction.

99.

I <u>Am</u> Perfect Samadhi,[57] the Truth and the Reality of No-"Difference", Which <u>Is</u> (Inherently Perfect) Consciousness <u>Itself</u>, Which Is Self-Existing, Self-Radiant, "Bright", One, Only, Non-Separate, and All Love-Bliss (<u>Itself</u>).

100.

Realize <u>Me</u> (by self-surrendering, self-forgetting, self-transcending, and always Me-Remembering, Me-

Invoking, and Me-Recognizing, heart-Contemplation of My bodily human Form, My Spiritual, and Always Blessing, Presence, and My Very, and Inherently Perfect, State).

101.

Live by My Darshan[58] (always Beholding Me), in constant Satsang (always Feasting on the Sight of Me).

102.

By Means of the Divine Grace Revealed by the Mere Sight (or Feel) of Me, Practice Ruchira Avatara Bhakti (which is self-surrendering, self-forgetting, and self-transcending devotion of body, feeling, attention, breath, and all of separate self to Me), and (by Means of the Divine Grace Revealed to that devotion) Practice Ruchira Avatara Seva[59] (which is active self-surrender, self-forgetting, and self-transcendence, via constant and Me-Remembering service to Me), and (by Means of the Divine Grace Revealed to that devotional service) Practice Ruchira Avatara Tapas[60] (which is self-discipline, in always self-surrendering, self-forgetting, and truly self-transcending devotional obedience and devotional conformity to Me).

103.

Therefore, in this Manner, and by the Divine Means of My Giving Grace and My Graceful Self-Revelation, Realize <u>Me</u> by heart, and by My "Bright" Infusion of your to-Me-surrendered body-mind.

104.

All This (That I have Herein Written), I Affirm by Heart (and <u>As</u> the Heart Itself).

105.

All This (That I have Hereby Affirmed), I Promise to the Heart (in every one, and all).

106.

Now (by This) I have Epitomized My summary (Written, and forever Speaking) Word of Heart.

107.

Therefore, surrender, forget, and transcend your separate and separative self by constant right (intelligent, self-disciplined, and truly devotionally responsive) obedience to My Word and Person, and (Thus) act only in accord (always) with My explicit Instructions (and, Thus, always only with My explicit Permission and Blessing), and (Thus, by this explicit devotion) Be Perfectly Simplified (by My Perfect Simplicity).

108.

This is the Heart-Word of the Ruchira Avatar, the Da Avatar, the Love-Ananda Avatar, Adi Da Samraj, the Divine World-Teacher,[61] the Divine Heart-Master, Who Is Da (the First and Original Person, the Source-Person, the One and Only, Non-Separate and Not "Different", Self of All and all), and Who Is Da Hridayam[62] (the One and Only Heart of All and all, in Whom all seeming-to-be-separate hearts Must Take Refuge, and, Thus and Thereby, Be Calmed of the Burning Heats of fear, sorrow, anger, un-love, and even all the seeking self-contractions of separative ego-"I"), and Who Is Da Love-Ananda (the Source, the Substance, the Gift, the Giver, and the Very Person of the "Bright" Divine Love-Bliss), and Who Is Da Avabhasa[63] (the Person of the "Bright" Itself, and the Very Giver of "Brightness"), and Who Is Santosha Da[64] (the "Bright" and Eternal and Always Already Non-Separate Person of Divine and Inherent Completeness, Divine Self-Satisfaction, Divine Self-Contentedness, or Perfect Searchlessness), Hereby Spoken in Extreme Simplicity for the Sake of all beings, in Love toward all beings, So That all beings may Awaken (by Means of My Giving Grace and My Graceful Self-Revelation) to the Only Truth That Sets the heart Free.

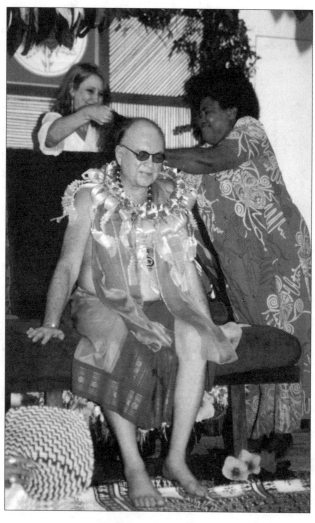

RUCHIRA AVATAR ADI DA SAMRAJ
Adidam Samrajashram (Naitauba), Fiji, 1997

PART THREE

Ruchira Avatara Bhakti Sara
(The Essence of Devotion To Me)

Ruchira Avatara Bhakti Sara
(The Essence of Devotion To Me)

1.

The only-by-Me Revealed and Given Way of Adidam (Which is the only-by-Me Revealed and Given Way of the Heart) is the devotional relationship to Me.

2.

The only-by-Me Revealed and Given Way of Adidam is not merely a system of self-applied techniques, or ego-centric practices, to be learned from Me and then applied to yourself, independent of Me

3.

The entire life of My devotee must be Ruchira Avatara Bhakti Yoga, or the always present-time devotional Yoga of direct (and directly and immediately ego-transcending) relationship to Me.

4.

True Religion, or Real-God-Yoga, is the practice of linking (or binding, or connecting, or "yoking") oneself to Reality Itself (Which Is Truth Itself, and the Only Real God).

5.

True Religion, or Real-God-Yoga, is the practice of consistently (and, Ultimately, Most Perfectly, and, therefore, Permanently) moving out of the disposition, and the presumption, and the very activity of separate and separative self, into the Love-Bliss-Full Condition of Oneness with That Which Is One, Whole, Absolute, All-Inclusive, and Beyond.

6.

Therefore, I Call My devotees to truly surrender themselves in devotional feeling-Contemplation of Me, by surrendering the principal faculties (of body, emotion, mind, and breath) to Me, moment to moment, and in all circumstances.

7.

The (moment to moment) surrender of the principal faculties to Me is the <u>Essence</u> of Ruchira Avatara Bhakti Yoga.

8.

Action engaged in the ordinary (or egoic) manner is (necessarily) conditional, and (inevitably) karmic (or ego-bound and ego-binding). Therefore, such ordinary (or egoic) action (necessarily, and inevitably) reinforces limitation and separateness. Because this is so, My devotees must understand that, if they continue to engage in action in the ordinary (or egoic) manner, they <u>will</u> <u>not</u> be truly (and most fully) En-Light-ened and Set Free by virtue of their mere "association" with Me. My devotees must actually <u>do</u> the counter-egoic Yoga of actively yielding the principal faculties of the body-mind to Me (moment to moment, and under all circumstances), through self-surrendering, self-forgetting, and (more and more) self-transcending feeling-Contemplation of Me.

9.

When they (thus) surrender the principal faculties of the body-mind to Me, My devotees are no longer devoted to action (in and of itself), and to the effects of action (in and of themselves), but they are (instead) truly transcending themselves in the midst of conditions, and they are (thereby) progressively (but entirely without seeking) being purified of the effects of action—only and entirely through Me-recognizing responsive devotion to Me.

10.

In the midst of daily living, and under all its various circumstances, there are demands on the body, demands on emotion, demands on mind, and demands on the breath. The conditions of existence make changes in all of the principal faculties, moment by moment. I Call My devotee to make Divine Yoga (or Freedom-"Bonding") out of each moment, by using body, emotion, mind, and breath in self-surrendering devotional feeling-Contemplation of Me.

11.

All the mechanisms that would, otherwise, automatically conform to the conditions of egoic life, or to conditionality altogether, must be turned to Me. Through that turning, My devotee becomes "yoked" (or Freedom-"Bonded") to Me.

12.

Therefore, My devotee must be responsible for the principal faculties of the body-mind, in every moment, and under all circumstances.

13.

Instead of wandering in the maze of thoughts, give Me the <u>faculty</u> of mind, which is epitomized by, and as, attention (itself).

14.

Instead of being tossed about by the waves of emotions, give Me the <u>faculty</u> of emotion, which is epitomized by, and as, feeling (itself).

15.

Instead of seeking bodily pleasure and avoiding bodily pain, turn the body toward Me, and, altogether, give Me the body, through full feeling-intention, enacted through constant devotional service to Me.

16.

The faculties of mind (or attention), emotion (or feeling), and body are connected to one another via the breath, and, thus, the gesture of surrender must also be done via the breath.

17.

Therefore, altogether, in the right and true practice of Ruchira Avatara Bhakti Yoga, mind (or attention), emotion (or feeling), and body are given over to Me, and breathed in heart-Communion with Me.

18.

The usual "method" of the ego, and, therefore, of ordinary people, is to become involved in what arises (whatever that may be in any particular circumstance), either by indulging in what arises or by avoiding what arises or by (otherwise) attempting to manipulate what arises. Such strategic effort in relation to what arises is not the Yoga of the only-by-Me Revealed and Given Way of Adidam, but it is merely the effort of the separate (and separative) self to struggle with itself.

19.

Even to strategically manipulate the separate (and separative) self (itself), in order to surrender the separate (and separative) self, is nothing but an (inevitably fruitless) effort of the separate (and separative) self to struggle with itself.

20.

Therefore, in the only-by-Me Revealed and Given Way of Adidam, self-surrender is not (in any sense) a strategic effort to do something to the separate (and separative) self. Rather, in the only-by-Me Revealed and Given Way of Adidam, self-surrender is the Me-recognizing, and, altogether, to-Me-Attracted, and to-Me-responsive (rather than strategically self-manipulative) giving of the fundamental faculties of the body-mind (which would, otherwise, be preoccupied with the separate and separative self) to <u>Me</u>, in every moment, and under all circumstances.

21.

Thus, the Secret of Ruchira Avatara Bhakti Yoga (and, therefore, of the entire Way of Adidam) is not to struggle with the <u>content</u> that is arising in and as the body-mind, but to <u>responsively</u> surrender the principal <u>faculties</u> of the body-mind to <u>Me</u>.

22.

It is always (in any moment) possible to responsively surrender the four fundamental faculties of the body-mind to Me, because (in and of themselves) these faculties stand prior to their "objects" (or apparent contents), and they are, therefore, never (themselves) bound to the egoic "program" of the moment. The mind may be thinking constantly, but the <u>faculty</u> of attention (itself) has no "object" or quality, and, therefore, it can, <u>itself</u>, always be responsively surrendered to Me. There may be reactive emotions arising, but the <u>faculty</u> of feeling is not (itself) qualified by any such "objects", and, therefore, it can, <u>itself</u>, always be responsively surrendered to Me. The condition of the body may, at any moment, be disturbance, or dis-ease, or lack of well-being, in one or another respect (or function, or organ), but the <u>faculty</u> of the body (itself, or in total, or as a whole) can, <u>itself</u>, always be responsively surrendered to Me. The cycle of the breath may be affected by forms of mind, reactive emotions, and bodily states, but the <u>faculty</u> of the breath is not (itself) identical to the ever-changing contents of the body-mind, and, therefore, it can, <u>itself</u>, always be responsively surrendered to Me.

23.

Taken all together, the four principal faculties of the body-mind account for <u>all</u> human functions.

24.

If any one (or a combination) of the four principal faculties is not rightly, truly, fully, and fully devotionally surrendered (responsively) to Me, and (thereby) brought into Communion with Me, then that faculty (or combination of faculties) reverts to the domain of egoity, and, therefore, to the contents of egoity. However, if My devotee always (responsively, devotionally) submits all four faculties (which are at the root of all aspects of human existence) directly to Me, then egoity (or ego-centricity, and self-contraction, and separativeness) is not reinforced, but it is (always presently) forgotten and (progressively) made obsolete.

25.

Thus, in the right, true, full, and fully devotional practice of Ruchira Avatara Bhakti Yoga, there is no struggle with separate (and separative) self.

26.

Because the four principal faculties are senior (or always prior) to their content, each of the four principal faculties of the body-mind is always available either to be <u>reactively</u> turned to its own apparent content or to be <u>responsively</u> turned to Me.

27.

Therefore, truly, there are <u>no</u> moments when responsive surrender of the separate (and separative) self is more difficult than in other moments—<u>unless</u> My devotee turns to (and identifies with) the apparent content of the separate (and separative) body-mind-self. If My devotee is simply Remembering Me (and recognizing Me, and responsively surrendering to Me), in <u>disposition</u>, and <u>intention</u>, and <u>action</u>, then the Yoga of Ruchira Avatara Bhakti is direct and (inherently) easy (or free of struggle with separate and separative self).

28.

My devotee who is rightly, truly, fully, and fully devotionally practicing the Yoga of Ruchira Avatara Bhakti does not, in any sense, <u>strategically</u> use (or seek with, or struggle with) the separate (and separative) self. Rather, My devotee who is rightly, truly, fully, and fully devotionally practicing the Yoga of Ruchira Avatara Bhakti makes the separate (and separative) self (itself) <u>obsolete</u>, by <u>not</u> <u>using</u> <u>it</u> (or, that is to say, by allowing the total body-mind, via its four principal faculties, to simply respond to Me)—until (in due course), through Ecstatic Absorption in (and, Ultimately, Perfect Identification with, and, Most Ultimately, Divine Realization of) Me, the separate (and separative) self utterly vanishes in Me.

29.

Therefore, always (responsively) turn to Me bodily.

30.

Always (responsively) turn to Me in feeling.

31.

Always (responsively) turn your attention to Me.

32.

Always (responsively) turn to Me by breathing Me (and allowing your body-mind to be "Breathed", and "Lived", by Me).

33.

This is the sadhana in the only-by-Me Revealed and Given Way of Adidam: <u>Always</u> (responsively) turn to <u>Me</u>—no matter what content, what sympathies, or what egoic "programs" arise.

34.

<u>Always</u> (responsively) turn <u>all</u> of the faculties of the body-mind to <u>Me</u>.

35.

<u>Always</u> (responsively) turn to <u>Me</u>, and (thus and thereby) surrender and forget yourself, rather than turn back on yourself (to see if anything is changing).

36.

That pure act of responsive devotional submission to Me, made in self-surrendering, self-forgetting, and (more and more) self-transcending feeling-Contemplation of Me, in every moment, <u>is</u> Ruchira Avatara Bhakti Yoga.

37.

To turn (responsively) to Me with each and all of the faculties of the body-mind is not self-contraction (or the avoidance of relationship), but, rather, it is the counter-egoic (and inherently self-forgetting) practice of Me-Consciousness, or devotional Communion with Me (and, Thus and Thereby, with the Divine Person).

38.

The "programs" of egoic habit do not persist unless you give them your energy and attention. If you give your energy and attention to <u>Me</u> (instead), then all your egoic "programs" will, Ultimately, become obsolete and (literally) vanish. That Is the Divine Truth and the Divine Law.

39.

You reinforce (or become) whatever you put your attention on (or to). Therefore, if you make <u>Me</u> the Object of your attention, all the other "things" of attention (which have no permanence) will dissolve.

40.

If you turn (responsively) to <u>Me</u>, the Virtue That I <u>Am</u> will Prove Itself. Therefore, I will Prove My Self to you, without your egoic effort, if you will do this simple (responsive, and inherently counter-egoic) turning to Me.

41.

The true fulfillment of the practice of Ruchira Avatara Bhakti Yoga is always a matter of My Giving Grace and My Graceful Self-Revelation.

42.

I Give (to each and to all) the Gift of the possibility of this devotional (and, Ultimately, Most Perfectly Liberating) relationship with Me.

43.

Devotion to Me is Inherently Love-Bliss-Full. To remember yourself is <u>not</u> Bliss, but stress and struggle. To Remember <u>Me</u>, and, as an inevitable consequence, to forget yourself, is to live in My Love-Bliss-Happiness.

44.

Therefore, whether you are in the beginning stages, the advancing stages, or the ultimate stages of the Way of Adidam, the essential practice is always the same devotional submission to Me, with all your parts, and the same Realizing of Me (and, Thus and Thereby, of Reality Itself, Which <u>Is</u> Truth Itself, or the Only Real God).

45.

True devotion to Me (or the right, true, full, and fully devotional practice of Ruchira Avatara Bhakti Yoga) is the Only Happiness, and the Only Freedom from the steel-hard mechanical and chemical bondage of suffering in which you are (otherwise) investing yourself.

46.

Therefore, Invoke Me, feel Me, breathe Me, and serve Me. Make no "room" for any "thing" else. That is what it is to be My true devotee.

47.

Thus, I Call all My formally acknowledged devotees to always (in every moment) turn <u>all</u> of the principal faculties of the body-mind to <u>Me</u>, rather than to the ego-act of self-contraction.

48.

Give Me that devotion (right, true, and full), and you will see Me Shining in My "Bright" Simplicity here.

49.

Then, by My Giving Grace and My Graceful Self-Revelation, you will (Ultimately, Most Perfectly) Realize Reality, or Truth, or Real God.

50.

My "Bright" and Omni-Present Divine Body and Presence and Person <u>Is</u> the only-by-Me Revealed and Given Way of Adidam (Which Is the Way of the Heart, Itself). I Must Give My Word of Heart-Instruction, for the Sake of all and All, but the Divine Way Itself Is simply <u>Me</u>—the One and Only and "Bright" Divine Person, Who <u>Is</u> Non-Separateness Itself, Appearing here before you without any limitations whatsoever.

51.

Therefore, Ruchira Avatara Bhakti Yoga is not an ego-based (or self-referring, or self-manipulating) practice of <u>strategic</u> surrender, but, rather, it is a <u>responsive</u> (or always Me-recognizing, to-Me-Attracted, and always presently, directly, and immediately ego-transcending) practice of <u>unconditional</u> surrender of separate (and separative) self to Me.

52.

The always present-time Circumstance of right, true, full, and fully devotional Ruchira Avatara Bhakti Yoga is Darshan (or Remembering, or even, if and when possible, direct physical sighting) of My Divinely "Bright" bodily (human) Form, and Darshan (or heart-"Locating") of My Divinely "Bright" (and All-and-all-Surrounding and All-and-all-Pervading) Divine Spiritual Body, and Darshan (or heart-Beholding, and heart-Realizing) of My Divine Person (the Divine Self-Condition and Source-Condition of all and All).

53.

Ruchira Avatara Bhakti Yoga is worship of <u>Me</u>, the "Bright" Itself, in <u>Person</u> (As My bodily human Form, My Spiritual, and Always Blessing, Presence, and My Very, and Inherently Perfect, State).

54.

Therefore, be My true devotee, and (thus) <u>always</u> (formally) practice Ruchira Avatara Bhakti Yoga (rightly, truly, fully, and fully devotionally), and be (thereby) Most Perfectly "Brightened" by <u>Me</u>.

RUCHIRA AVATAR ADI DA SAMRAJ
Adidam Samrajashram (Naitauba), Fiji, 1997

EPILOGUE

What Will you Do
If you Love Me?

What Will you Do
If you Love Me?

The only-by-Me Revealed and Given Way of Adidam (Which is the only-by-Me Revealed and Given Way of the Heart) is the Way of those who love Me. The Principle of devotional surrender to Me is the Principal, Fundamental, and Inherently Complete Discipline of the Way of Adidam (or the Way of the Heart). All the forms of functional, practical, relational, and cultural self-discipline I Give to them are always readily embraced, with gratitude, by My true devotees, simply because I have Instructed them to do so. And, in the case of My true devotees who embrace <u>all</u> the by Me Revealed and Given functional, practical, relational, and cultural disciplines of the total (or full and complete) practice of the Way of Adidam, all the potential esoteric Revelations that may (or, otherwise, must) occur in the course of the progressive Great Process of the Way of Adidam,[65] and all the potential Excellences of Divine Self-Realization in the Great Fulfillment of the Way of Adidam, appear spontaneously and naturally to them, by My Grace, because they each turn their attention, and feeling, and body, and breath to Me at <u>all</u> times, and because they each perform <u>all</u> activities as instants of Love-Communion with Me.

<u>All</u> My devotees must embrace all the practices of devotion, service, self-discipline, and meditation that I Give to them. Nevertheless, the <u>principal</u> capability of the

human being (or of any other conditionally manifested being) is that of distraction and attachment, rather than mere self-restraint. Therefore, the Principle, or Great Mover, of the only-by-Me Revealed and Given practice of the Way of Adidam is not discipline itself, but Distraction by Me and Attachment to Me. Because they love Me, My true devotees adapt all their life-activities to the "radically" direct Way of devotional surrender and devotional conformity to Me.

The principal characteristic of My true devotees is that they are Distracted by Me and Attached to Me. They find Me to be the Greatest of all distractions. Therefore, they need not make any effort to be constantly Attached to Me. They naturally Remember Me at all times. They only think about Me, talk about Me, and listen to others tell Leelas (or Stories) about Me. They study My Wisdom-Teaching, they embrace My disciplines, but, even more, they are profoundly and intensively absorbed in My Person, My Gestures, My Play with all and All.

In this Manner, those who love Me are gradually relieved of the distracting power of ordinary things, experiences, relations, desires, and thoughts. Ultimately, if they embrace the right, true, full, and fully devotional practice of the Way of Adidam, I Distract My true devotees from all and All. Thus, their intensive and exclusive Attachment to Me leads My true devotees, first, to right, true, full, and fully devotional practice of the Way Revealed and Given by Me, and, Ultimately, to Most Perfect Realization of My Self-Existing and Self-Radiant Divine Self-Condition of All-and-all-Including and All-and-all-Transcending Love-Bliss.

I have Come to Waken the entire world through My Heart-Word, and My Demands, and the Mere Presence of My "Bright" Person. The entire world would do well to listen to Me and take up the responsible practice of the only-by-Me Revealed and Given Way of Adidam. Nevertheless, I have Come to do more than Communicate a Wisdom-Teaching to the wallydraigle world. I have Come to Live (now, and forever hereafter) with those who love Me with ego-overwhelming love, and I have Come to Love them likewise Overwhelmingly. If there is not this ego-overwhelming love of Me (Who Loves All and all, Overwhelmingly), then the Great Awakening will forever be postponed by pious self-attentions and the forever sessioning "talking" school of ego-based, and ego-gesturing, religiosity.

Those who would hear Me and see Me must take up the Way of Adidam as formal members of either the first congregation or the second congregation of the great community of all My formally acknowledged devotees. Only My formally acknowledged first and second congregation devotees embrace all the by Me Revealed and Given functional, practical, relational, and cultural disciplines of the only-by-Me Revealed and Given Way of Adidam. And all My true devotees in either the first congregation or the second congregation of formal approach to Me embrace the total practice of the Way of Adidam entirely and only as a Process of self-transcending Love-Communion with Me. Therefore, by My Grace alone, My true devotees grow to understand themselves, and, by transcending themselves in Me, they transcend the world.

But the Motive of My true devotees is not the disciplines, nor mystical experience, nor philosophy. My true devotees practice the Way of Adidam because they love Me. They have no personal (or inherent) capability to utterly turn away from the world, or to utterly transcend themselves. Therefore, I have Come to Live with them (now, and forever hereafter). When My devotees Find Me, the same weakness that led them to distraction by all the merely binding and passing possibilities of this mummery-world, and to attachment to the possible experiences of its indifferent maze of mere patterns patterning, becomes the very capability that makes possible their Liberation into My Eternal "Bright" Domain of Love-Bliss. Thus, because I Am the Ultimate and Most Absorbing "Object" of their inherent weakness, I Distract My devotees to Me, away

from all the mummery of possible experiences and endings. They become Attached to Me by the power of their
own tendency to distraction. Therefore, even their own
(and, otherwise, binding) power of desire leads them to
the Ecstasy of egoless heart-Communion with Me, because
they love Me.

I Am the Self-Existing and Self-Radiant Divine Self-
Consciousness Itself, the One and Only and Non-Separate
and Indivisible and Indestructible "Bright" Self-Condition
and Source-Condition of all and All, Appearing in bodily
(human) Avataric-Incarnation-Form for the Sake of all and
All. Those who love Me most profoundly, who are might-
ily Distracted by Me and most happily Attached to Me, and
who cannot profoundly entertain any desires or thoughts
other than their love of Me, are most easily turned from
themselves. Divine Ecstasy, or Real-God-Communion, is
natural to them, because I have been Born, and because I
have (Thus and Thereby) Revealed and Given, to all and
All, the Real Divine Forms That make It possible for any
and every conditionally manifested being to Worship Me
and to Realize Me. Thus, by My own Self-Power, of Inherent Attractiveness, I Distract My true devotees to My Self,
and I Draw them into My own Divine Self-Condition and
Self-"Bright" Domain.

My lovers, My true devotees, simply love Me. That is
the Summation of their recognition-response to Me. They
appear to understand a little of My Wisdom-Teaching, but
they do not depend on "inward" practices, or on mystical
experiences, or on any turn of events. The only-by-Me
Revealed and Given Way of Adidam is fulfilled by their
mere Attachment to Me—since that Attachment is so
mighty that they have no binding attention left over for
ordinary reactions and seeking pursuits, nor are they
egoically overwhelmed by the phenomena of esoteric
meditation. They simply love Me. They live in constant
Remembrance of Me, and in constant loving service to Me.
Every moment of their lives is simply a moment of Love-

Communion with Me. Therefore, they are Granted perpetual Ecstasy by Me, in the Form of self-forgetting Love-Communion with Me, the Self-Existing and Self-Radiant Divine "Bright" Person of Love-Bliss.

My special Mission is to Live with such true devotees. I have always Looked for them. I always Test every one, to see who are My true lovers. I wait. Many surround Me in My Place. Many come to Me and listen to Me and practice all around Me. Many turn to Me with the good heart. But those who love Me best will, Ultimately, Realize Me Most Perfectly, by overwhelming Attachment to Me in Person.

My true lovers are the cause of My Birth. They are the cause that keeps Me Alive, even after My Teaching Demonstration and My Full Divine Self-Revelation Are Complete and My Full Heart-Word Is Fully Given—and all My true lovers (now, and forever hereafter) will, simply by their Me-Remembering and Me-Recognizing love of Me, keep Me Alive in Divine Person forever, even after My Time of Physical Avataric Incarnation Is Past. My true devotees (now, and forever hereafter) Are (and will always Be) Blessed by Me, to Find Me Alive As the Personal Love-Bliss-Presence That Is the Divine Reality and Truth of the ever-Playing world.

The Essence of the daily practice of My devotees is the Ecstasy of Love-Communion with Me. One who loves Me accepts every moment of experience as My conditionally manifested Form. Whatever arises, he or she accepts it as My "Bright" Form, My Divine Play. My true devotee simply loves Me, Communes with Me in every instant, constantly serves Me with the entire body-mind (no matter what arises), and accepts every moment of experience As My "Bright" Form. In this manner, My true devotee never presumes himself or herself to be separated from Me. My true devotee is always in love with Me.

Those who are most profoundly Distracted by Me grow (by My Grace) to see Only Me in every thing, every one, and every event. But no form, or person, or event has power in itself to distract My true lovers from Me. They see <u>Me</u> in all experiences, all persons, all events. Therefore, they are not distracted by experiences, or persons, or events. They are Distracted by <u>Me</u>.

Now, and forever hereafter, each and all of My formally acknowledged devotees will be Blessed, by Me, to devotionally recognize Me, and, thus, to respond devotionally to Me, and, by Means of that devotion, to Remember Me, and to Find Me, and (potentially, within the first congregation or the second congregation of formal approach to Me) to Realize Me Most Perfectly. And I will, forever, Serve that devotional recognition and response to Me, and That Remembering of Me, and That Finding of Me, and That Realizing of Me—through the by-Me-Given Means of all My formally acknowledged Instruments and all My formally acknowledged Agents, including My by-Me-Given (Written, and Spoken) Wisdom-Teaching, and all Kinds of True (photographic, and otherwise technically, or even artistically, rendered) Representations (or Icons, or Murtis) of Me, and all the Recorded Leelas (or Stories) of My History and Play with My devotees, and all My by-Me-Empowered Sanctuaries, and all My by-Me-Empowered Sacred Things, and the Collective of all My True Devotee-Instruments, and My (in every then present-time) formally acknowledged "Living Murti" (or specially formally Appointed human Blessing-Agent of Me-Contemplation).

Now, and forever hereafter, all My formally acknowledged devotees are Called, by Me, to the Ecstasy of Love-Communion with Me, and I will, forever, Reveal That Ecstasy to all via the love My most intimate true devotees demonstrate toward Me. Therefore, because there are true devotees, who truly love Me in the Great Manner, while I Am Present here in bodily (human) Form, and because there will forever be such true devotees of Mine (for I will remain Transcendentally, Spiritually, Divinely, and, altogether, Really and Tangibly Present here, always and forever, after the physical Lifetime of My bodily human

Form)—all My devotees who truly love Me and formally resort to Me, in all the times after the physical death of My bodily (human) Form, will be served by My true devotees, so that, forever, all My formally acknowledged devotees will be thus enabled to Find Me and to Realize Me.

Forever after the physical death of My bodily (human) Form, the ever-patterning world of temporary experience remains, but My gathering of formally acknowledged devotees also remains. Therefore, now, and forever hereafter, those who associate with My formally acknowledged true lovers will also, by Means of the example (and the formal Instrumentality) of My thus true devotees, be Moved to Me, and, altogether, responsively turned to Me, with profoundly Distracted true love.

I will always Bless all My formally acknowledged devotees, now, and forever hereafter, and, after the physical death of My bodily (human) Form, I will continue to Bless all of them, just as I do while I Am Present in bodily (human) Form. Forever, every one will call on Me in the company of My true lovers, and I will Always Be Truly Present, every then and there.

I __Am__ the One and Only, Non-Separate and Indivisible, Self-Existing and Indestructible, Self-Radiant and Eternally "Bright" Person, the Divine Self-Condition and Source-Condition of all and All, forever Surrounding all and All, and forever Pervading all and All, and forever Beyond all and All.

Truly, now, and forever hereafter, only those who love Me can formally approach Me and most fruitfully listen to Me, and only those who formally embrace right, true, full, and fully devotional practice of the Way of Adidam can grow to hear Me and to see Me and to Most Perfectly Realize Me.

Some of My devotees are, at first, most involved in right understanding of My Teaching Arguments and in responsible practice of the forms of self-discipline I have Given to all My devotees, while others are always, from the beginning, naturally more capable of Distraction by Me and Attachment to Me. Therefore, some of My devotees practice self-discipline and love Me, while others of My devotees simply love Me, and the forms of self-discipline develop readily in their case, as if without any effort of application on their part. Some of My devotees mature in love of Me by stages. Others of My devotees simply love Me from the beginning. At last, even the most disciplined or experienced of My devotees simply loves Me.

I Am the Self-Existing and Self-Radiant "Bright" Divine Reality, Truth, and Person, the Divine Liberator of those who love Me and surrender to Me in countless acts of love. I Am the Method and the Guide. I Am the Living Truth of the world.

All religions are historical forms of the Single and Ancient Way of Distracted love for the Divine Person, especially as Revealed in the Life and in the Company and in the Person of Incarnate Adepts, or Realizers, in their various degrees and stages of Realization. This is the Great Secret. And This Is My Revelation to you: I Am, In and As My Avataric-Incarnation-Form, the First, the Last, and the Only Adept-Realizer, Adept-Revealer, and Adept-Revelation of Most Perfect (or seventh stage) Divine Enlightenment. Aham Da Asmi. I Am Da, the Only One Who Is, the Very and Only Person That Is to Be Realized by all and All. Therefore, love Me As My Avataric-Incarnation-Form, and (Thus and Thereby) love Me As I Am, and As the constant Form and Condition of all your experience. I Am That Which Is Always Already The Case. I Am the Non-Separate and Only One, the "Bright" One, the Indivisible and Indestructible One, Who Is all and All. Therefore, surrender Only to Me, and accept all your experience As My own Play. If you do This, you will be constantly free of all seeking attachment (and all aversion, or counter-seeking reaction) to any and every psycho-physical experience (or all conditionally manifested experiences). Therefore, even all possible experience will only and simply increase your direct (or always present-time, or non-seeking, and non-binding, but always only Me-Finding, and you-Liberating) Attachment to Me.

All experience (in itself) only binds you to your own body-mind—unless you are established in self-transcending (Ecstatic, or self-contraction-transcending) love of Me, the Only One Who Is. Therefore, if you love Me, become My formally acknowledged devotee, and, as My formally acknowledged devotee, enter (thus) Freely (or non-bindingly) into the Play of experience (always in self-surrendering and self-forgetting heart-Communion with Me, and always with your total body-mind conformed to Me through the constant maintaining of the functional, practical, relational, and cultural self-disciplines that are your obligation, by eternal vow to Me, in the only-by-Me Revealed and Given Way of Adidam). In this manner, serve Me in My Avataric-Incarnation-Form, and serve Me As I Am, and serve Me in all circumstances and in all relationships. If you love Me thusly, you will cease to continue in the willful and egoically "self-possessed" (or self-absorbed)[66] path of your preferential desires, and, by My Grace, you will be purified of egoity, of self-contraction, of egoic reaction, and of every kind of accumulated egoic habit, and of every kind of seeker's self-indulgence.

If you truly love Me, it is because I have Shown you Who I Am. Therefore, by Means of right, true, full, and fully devotional love of Me, you will Come to Me, Where I Am. Most Ultimately, if you are My true, and fully practicing, devotee, you will, by My Grace, Realize Me, because you love Me.

You become (or take the form of) what your attention most really moves upon. Therefore, if I Am your Beloved, your love-attention will cause you to Realize Indivisible Unity with Me.

Until you fall in love, love is what you fear to do. When you have fallen in love, and you are (thus) always already in love, then you cease to fear to love—you cease to be reluctant to surrender, and to be self-forgetful and foolish, and to be single-minded, and to suffer an "other". Those who fall in love with Me Fall into Me. Those whose hearts are given, in love, to Me, Fall into My Heart. Those who are Mine, because they are in love with Me, no longer demand to be fulfilled through conditional experience and through the survival (or perpetuation) of the ego-"I". Their love for Me grants them Access to Me, and, Thus, to My Love-Bliss, because I <u>Am</u> Love-Ananda, the Divine Love-Bliss, in Person.

What will My lover do but love Me? I suffer every form and condition of every one who loves Me, because I Love My devotee <u>As</u> My own Form, My own Condition. I Love My devotee <u>As</u> the One by Whom <u>I</u> Am Distracted.

I Grant all My own Divine and "Bright" Excesses to those who love Me, in exchange for all their doubts and sufferings. Those who "Bond" themselves to Me, through love-surrender, are inherently Free of fear and wanting need. They transcend the ego-"I" (the cause of all conditional experience), and they (cause and all and All) Dissolve in Me, for I <u>Am</u> the Heart of all and All, and I <u>Am</u> the Heart Itself, and the Heart Itself <u>Is</u> the Only Reality, Truth, and Real God of All and all.

What is a Greater Message than This?

Notes to the Text of the
DA LOVE-ANANDA GITA
(THE FREE GIFT OF THE DIVINE LOVE-BLISS)

Part One

1. Avatar Adi Da Samraj spontaneously Gave the Name "Adidam" in January 1996. This primary Name for the Way He has Revealed and Given is simply His own Principal Name ("Adi Da") with the addition of "m" at the end. When He first Gave this Name, Adi Da Samraj pointed out that the final "m" adds a mantric force, evoking the effect of the primal Sanskrit syllable "Om". (For Avatar Adi Da's Revelation of the most profound esoteric significance of "Om" as the Divine Sound of His own Very Being, see *He-and-She Is Me—The Seventeen Companions Of The True Dawn Horse, Book Seven: The Indivisibility Of Consciousness and Light In The Divine Body Of The Ruchira Avatar.*) Simultaneously, the final "m" suggests the English word "Am" (expressing "I Am"), such that the Name "Adidam" also evokes Avatar Adi Da's Primal Self-Confession, "I Am Adi Da", or, more simply, "I Am Da" (or "Aham Da Asmi").

2. The technical term "consider" or "consideration" in Avatar Adi Da's Wisdom-Teaching means a process of one-pointed but ultimately thoughtless concentration and exhaustive contemplation of something until its ultimate obviousness is clear. As engaged in the Way of Adidam, "consideration" is not merely an intellectual investigation. It is the participatory investment of one's whole being. If one "considers" something fully in the context of one's practice of feeling-Contemplation of Avatar Adi Da Samraj, this concentration results "in both the highest intuition and the most practical grasp of the Lawful and Divine necessities of human existence".

3. Avatar Adi Da uses "Self-Existing and Self-Radiant" to indicate the two fundamental aspects of the One Divine Person—Existence (or Being, or Consciousness) Itself, and Radiance (or Energy, or Light) Itself.

4. For Avatar Adi Da's further commentaries on the *Bhagavad Gita*, see "The Tree of Light Is Above the Head, and I Shine Forever In The Sky Beyond It", in Part Three of *Hridaya Rosary (Four Thorns Of Heart-Instruction)—The Five Books Of The Heart Of The Adidam Revelation, Book Four: The "Late-Time" Avataric Revelation Of The*

Universally Tangible Divine Spiritual Body, Which Is The Supreme Agent Of The Great Means To Worship and To Realize The True and Spiritual Divine Person (The egoless Personal Presence Of Reality and Truth, Which Is The Only Real God), and "The Explicit Teaching of the *Bhagavad Gita* and Its Ultimate (Secret) Import" (in *The Basket Of Tolerance—The Seventeen Companions Of The True Dawn Horse, Book Seventeen: The Perfect Guide To Perfectly Unified Understanding Of The One and Great Tradition Of Mankind, and Of The Divine Way Of Adidam As The Perfect Completing Of The One and Great Tradition Of Mankind).*

5. The entire practice of the Way of Adidam is founded in heart-recognition of Ruchira Avatar Adi Da Samraj as the Very Divine Being in Person.

AVATAR ADI DA SAMRAJ: The only-by-Me Revealed and Given Way of Adidam (Which is the only-by-Me Revealed and Given Way of the Heart) is the Way of life you live when you rightly, truly, fully, and fully devotionally recognize Me, and when, on that basis, you rightly, truly, fully, and fully devotionally respond to Me.

. . . In responsive devotional recognition of Me, the principal faculties are loosed from the objects to which they are otherwise bound—loosed from the patterns of self-contraction. The faculties turn to Me, and, in that turning, there is tacit recognition of Me, tacit experiential Realization of Me, of Happiness Itself, of My Love-Bliss-Full Condition. That "Locating" of Me opens the body-mind spontaneously. When you have been thus Initiated by Me, it then becomes your responsibility, your sadhana, to continuously Remember Me, to constantly return to this recognition of Me, in which you are Attracted to Me, in which you respond to Me spontaneously with all the principal faculties. ("Recognize My Divine Body and 'Bright' Person, and Let Everything Melt That Is 'Between' You and Me", in *Hridaya Rosary*)

6. By the word "Bright" (and its variations, such as "Brightness"), Avatar Adi Da refers to the eternally, infinitely, and inherently Self-Radiant Divine Being, the Being of Indivisible and Indestructible Light. As Adi Da Writes in His Spiritual Autobiography, *The Knee Of Listening—The Seventeen Companions Of The True Dawn Horse, Book Four: The Early-Life Ordeal and The "Radical" Spiritual Realization Of The Ruchira Avatar*:

. . . from my earliest experience of life I have Enjoyed a Condition that, as a child, I called the "Bright".

I have always known desire, not merely for extreme pleasures of the senses and the mind, but for the highest Enjoyment of Spiritual Power and Mobility. But I have not been seated in desire, and desire has only been a play that I have grown to understand and enjoy with-out conflict. I have always been Seated in the "Bright".

Even as a baby I remember only crawling around inquisitively with a boundless Feeling of Joy, Light, and Freedom in the middle of my head that was bathed in Energy moving unobstructed in a Circle, down from above, all the way down, then up, all the way up, and around again, and always Shining from my heart. It was an Expanding Sphere of Joy from the heart. And I was a Radiant Form, the Source of Energy, Love-Bliss, and Light in the midst of a world that is entirely Energy, Love-Bliss, and Light. I was the Power of Reality, a direct Enjoyment and Communication of the One Reality. I was the Heart Itself, Who Lightens the mind and all things. I was the same as every one and every thing, except it became clear that others were apparently unaware of the "Thing" Itself.

Even as a little child I recognized It and Knew It, and my life was not a matter of anything else. That Awareness, that Conscious Enjoyment, that Self-Existing and Self-Radiant Space of Infinitely and inherently Free Being, that Shine of inherent Joy Standing in the heart and Expanding from the heart, is the "Bright". And It is the entire Source of True Humor. It is Reality. It is not separate from anything.

7. Avatar Adi Da uses the phrase "Most Perfect(ly)" in the sense of "Absolutely Perfect(ly)". Similarly, the phrase "Most Ultimate(ly)" is equivalent to "Absolutely Ultimate(ly)". "Most Perfect(ly)" and "Most Ultimate(ly)" are always references to the seventh (or Divinely Enlightened) stage of life. (See note 22.)

8. The fundamental self-contraction, or the sense of separate and separative existence.

9. Avatar Adi Da uses the term "bond", when lowercased, to refer to the process by which the egoic individual (already presuming separateness, and, therefore, bondage to the separate self) attaches itself karmically to the world of others and things through the constant search for self-fulfillment. In contrast, when He capitalizes the term "Bond", Avatar Adi Da is making reference to the process of His devotee's devotional "Bonding" to Him, which process is the Great Means for transcending all forms of limited, or karmic, "bonding".

10. In this context, Adi Da Samraj is using the term "gross" in reference to the structure of the human body-mind and its environment. He Describes conditional existence as having three dimensions—gross, subtle, and causal.

The gross, or physical, dimension of conditional existence is associated with the physical body and experience in the waking state.

The subtle dimension, which is senior to and pervades the gross dimension, includes the etheric (or energetic), lower mental (or verbal-intentional and lower psychic), and higher mental (or deeper psychic, mystical, and discriminative) functions, and is associated with experience in the dreaming state. In the human psycho-physical structure, the subtle dimension is primarily associated with the ascending energies of the spine, the brain core, and the subtle centers of mind in the higher brain.

The causal dimension is senior to and pervades both the gross and the subtle dimensions. It is the root of attention, or the essence of the separate and separative ego-"I". The causal dimension is associated with the right side of the heart, specifically with the sinoatrial node, or "pacemaker" (the psycho-physical source of the heartbeat). Its corresponding state of consciousness is the formless awareness of deep sleep.

For Avatar Adi Da's discussion of the gross, subtle, and causal dimensions, see *Santosha Adidam—The Seventeen Companions Of The True Dawn Horse, Book Fourteen: The Essential Summary Of The Divine Way Of Adidam*, Part One, section III.

11. Avatar Adi Da Samraj is the "Avataric Incarnation", or the Divinely Descended Embodiment, of the Divine Person. The reference "Avataric Incarnation" indicates that Avatar Adi Da Samraj fulfills both the traditional expectation of the East—that the True God-Man is an Avatar, or an utterly Divine "Descent" of Real God in conditionally manifested form—and the traditional expectations of the West—that the True God-Man is an Incarnation, or an utterly human Embodiment of Real God.

For Avatar Adi Da's discussion of the "Avatar" and "Incarnation" traditions, and of His unique and all-Completing Role as the "Avataric Incarnation" of the Divine Person, see "'Avatar' and 'Incarnation': The Complementary God-Man Traditions of East and West", in *The Truly Human New World-Culture Of Unbroken Real-God-Man—The Seventeen Companions Of The True Dawn Horse, Book Two: The Eastern Versus The Western Traditional Cultures Of Mankind, and The Unique New Non-Dual Culture Of The True World-Religion Of Adidam*.

12. The Tantric traditions of India and the Himalayas describe as "heroic" the practice of an individual whose impulse to Liberation and commitment to his or her Guru are so strong that all circumstances of life, even those traditionally considered inauspicious for Spiritual practice (such as consumption of intoxicants and sexual activity), can be rightly made use of as part of the Spiritual process.

Avatar Adi Da's uniquely "Heroic" Ordeal, however, was undertaken not (primarily) for the sake of His own Liberation, but in order to discover, through His own experience, what is necessary for all beings to Realize the Truth. Because of His utter Freedom from egoic bondage and egoic karmas, Avatar Adi Da's Sadhana was "Heroic" in a manner that had never previously been possible and will never again be possible for any other being. As the Divine Person, it was necessary for Him to have experienced the entire gamut of human seeking, in order for Him to be able to Teach any and all that came to Him.

Avatar Adi Da has Instructed that, because of His unique "Heroic" Demonstration, His devotees can simply practice the Way He has Revealed and Given, and are not to attempt the (in any case impossible) task of duplicating His Ordeal.

13. With the phrase "the 'dark' time of mortality" Avatar Adi Da is referring not to a particular period of time but to the confrontation with the mortality of everyone and everything conditional.

14. On January 11, 1986, Avatar Adi Da passed through a profound Yogic Swoon, which He later described as the initial Event of His Divine "Emergence". Avatar Adi Da's Divine "Emergence" is an ongoing Process in which His bodily (human) Form has been (and is ever more profoundly and potently being) conformed to Himself, the Very Divine Person, such that His bodily (human) Form is now (and forever hereafter) an utterly Unobstructed Sign and Agent of His own Divine Being.

For Avatar Adi Da's Revelation of the significance of His Divine "Emergence", see *The Dawn Horse Testament Of The Ruchira Avatar: The "Testament Of Secrets" Of The Divine World-Teacher, Ruchira Avatar Adi Da Samraj* or *The Heart Of The Dawn Horse Testament Of The Ruchira Avatar—The Seventeen Companions Of The True Dawn Horse, Book Twelve: The Epitome Of The "Testament Of Secrets" Of The Divine World-Teacher, Ruchira Avatar Adi Da Samraj*, Part One, "The True Dawn Horse Is The Only Way To Me", section III.

15. "Leela" is Sanskrit for "play", or "sport". In many religious and Spiritual traditions, all of conditionally manifested existence is regarded to be the Leela (or the Divine Play, Sport, or Free Activity) of the Divine Person. "Leela" also means the Awakened Play of a Realized Adept of any degree, through which he or she mysteriously Instructs and Liberates others and Blesses the world itself. By extension, a Leela is an instructive and inspiring story of such an Adept's Teaching and Blessing Play.

16. "Difference" is the epitome of the egoic presumption of separateness—in contrast with the Realization of Oneness, or Non-"Difference", that is native to Spiritual and Transcendental Divine Self-Consciousness.

17. In the context of Divine Enlightenment in the seventh stage of life in the Way of Adidam, the Spiritual process continues. Avatar Adi Da has uniquely Revealed the four phases of the seventh stage process: Divine Transfiguration, Divine Transformation, Divine Indifference, and Divine Translation.

Divine Translation is the most ultimate "Event" of the entire process of Divine Awakening. Avatar Adi Da Describes Divine Translation as the Outshining of all noticing of objective conditions, through the infinitely magnified Force of Consciousness Itself. Divine Translation is the Outshining of all destinies, wherein there is no return to the conditional realms.

For Avatar Adi Da's extended Discussion of Divine Translation, see *The All-Completing and Final Divine Revelation To Mankind— The Seventeen Companions Of The True Dawn Horse, Book Eleven: A Summary Description Of The Supreme Yoga Of The Seventh Stage Of Life In The Divine Way Of Adidam*, Part Two (or *The Dawn Horse Testament Of The Ruchira Avatar*, chapter forty-four).

18. Avatar Adi Da Affirms that there is a Divine Self-Domain that is the Perfectly Subjective Condition of the conditional worlds. It is not "elsewhere", not an objective "place" (like a subtle "heaven" or mythical "paradise"), but It is the always present, Transcendental, Inherently Spiritual, Divine Source-Condition of every conditionally manifested being and thing. Avatar Adi Da Reveals that the Divine Self-Domain is not other than the Divine Heart Itself, Who He Is. To Realize the seventh stage of life (by the Grace of Avatar Adi Da Samraj) is to Awaken to the Divine Self-Domain.

19. Avatar Adi Da Samraj frequently Describes His Blessing-Power as being like a kiln. In a kiln, as the wet clay objects are heated more and more, they begin to glow. Eventually, the kiln is so hot that everything within it glows with a white light, and the definitions of the individual objects dissolve in the brightness. Just so, as a devotee matures in Avatar Adi Da's Spiritual Company, all presumptions of separateness as an apparently individual ego-"I" are more and more Outshined by the "Brightness" of His Divine Person and Blessing.

Part Two

20. The Sanskrit phrase "Aham Da Asmi" means "I (Aham) Am (Asmi) Da". The Name "Da", meaning "the One Who Gives", indicates that Avatar Adi Da Samraj is the Supreme Divine Giver, the Avataric Incarnation of the Very Divine Person.

Avatar Adi Da's Declaration "Aham Da Asmi" is similar in form to the "Mahavakyas", or "Great Statements", of ancient India (found in the Upanishads, the collected esoteric Instruction of ancient Gurus). However, the significance of "Aham Da Asmi" is fundamentally different from that of the traditional Mahavakyas. Each of the Upanishadic Mahavakyas expresses, in a few words, the profound (though not most ultimate) degree of Realization achieved by great Realizers of the past. For example, the Upanishadic Mahavakya "Aham Brahmasmi" ("I Am Brahman") expresses a great individual's Realization that he or she is Identified with the Divine Being (Brahman), and is not, in Truth, identified with his or her apparently individual body-mind. However, "Aham Da Asmi", rather than being a proclamation of a human being who has devoted his or her life most intensively to the process of Real-God-Realization and has thereby Realized the Truth to an extraordinarily profound degree, is Avatar Adi Da's Confession that He Is the Very Divine Person, Da, Who has Appeared here in bodily (human) Form, in order to Reveal Himself to all and All, for the sake of the Divine Liberation of all and All.

21. The Name "Love-Ananda" combines both English ("Love") and Sanskrit ("Ananda", meaning "Bliss"), thus bridging the West and the East, and communicating Avatar Adi Da's Function as the Divine World-Teacher. The combination of "Love" and "Ananda" means "the Divine Love-Bliss". The Name "Love-Ananda" was given to Avatar Adi Da by His principal human Spiritual Master, Swami Muktananda, who spontaneously conferred it upon Avatar Adi Da in 1969. However, Avatar Adi Da did not use the Name "Love-Ananda" until April 1986, after the Great Event that Initiated His Divine "Emergence". (See note 14.)

22. Avatar Adi Da has Revealed the underlying structure of human growth in seven stages.

The first three stages of life develop, respectively, the physical, emotional, and mental/volitional functions of the body-mind. The first stage begins at birth and continues for approximately five to seven years; the second stage follows, continuing until approximately the age of twelve to fourteen; and the third stage is optimally complete by the early twenties. In the case of virtually all individuals, however, failed adaptation in the earlier stages of life means that maturity in the third stage of life takes much longer to attain, and it is usually never fulfilled, with the result that the ensuing stages of Spiritual development do not even begin.

In the Way of Adidam, however, growth in the first three stages of life unfolds in the Spiritual Company of Avatar Adi Da and is based in the practice of feeling-Contemplation of His bodily (human) Form and in devotion, service, and self-discipline in relation to His bodily (human) Form. By the Grace of this relationship to Avatar Adi Da, the first three (or foundation) stages of life are lived and fulfilled in a self-transcending devotional disposition, or (as He Describes it) "in the 'original' or beginner's devotional context of the fourth stage of life".

The fourth stage of life is the transitional stage between the gross, bodily-based point of view of the first three stages of life and the subtle, psychic point of view of the fifth stage of life. The fourth stage of life is the stage of Spiritual devotion, or surrender of separate self, in which the gross functions of the being are submitted to the higher psychic, or subtle, functions of the being, and, through these psychic functions, to the Divine. In the fourth stage of life, the gross, or bodily-based, personality of the first three stages of life is purified through reception of the Spiritual Force ("Holy Spirit", or "Shakti") of the Divine Reality, Which prepares the being to out-grow the bodily-based point of view.

In the Way of Adidam, as the orientation of the fourth stage of life matures, heart-felt surrender to the bodily (human) Form of Avatar Adi Da deepens by His Grace, drawing His devotee into Love-Communion with His All-Pervading Spiritual Presence. Growth in the "basic" context of the fourth stage of life in the Way of the Heart is also characterized by a Baptizing Current of Spirit-Energy that is at first felt to flow down the front of the body from above the head to the bodily base.

The Descent of Avatar Adi Da's Spirit-Baptism releases obstructions predominantly in the waking, or frontal, personality. This frontal Yoga purifies His devotee and infuses him or her with His Spirit-Power. Avatar Adi Da's devotee is awakened to profound love of and devotional intimacy with Him.

If the transition to the sixth stage of life is not otherwise made at maturity in the "basic" context of the fourth stage of life, the Spirit-Current is felt to turn about at the bodily base and ascend to the brain core, and the fourth stage of life matures to its "advanced" context, which involves the ascent of Avatar Adi Da's Spiritual Blessing and purifies the spinal line of the body-mind.

In the fifth stage of life, attention is concentrated in the subtle, or psychic, levels of awareness in ascent. The Spirit-Current is felt to penetrate the brain core and rise toward the Matrix of Light and Love-Bliss infinitely above the crown of the head, possibly culminating in the temporary experience of fifth stage conditional Nirvikalpa Samadhi, or "formless ecstasy". In the Way of Adidam, most practitioners will not need to practice in the context of the fifth stage of life, but will rather be Awakened, by Adi Da's Grace, from maturity in the fourth stage of life to the Witness-Position of Consciousness (in the context of the sixth stage of life).

In the traditional development of the sixth stage of life, attention is inverted upon the essential self and the Perfectly Subjective Position of Consciousness, to the exclusion of conditional phenomena. In the Way of Adidam, however, the deliberate intention to invert attention for the sake of Realizing Transcendental Consciousness does not characterize the sixth stage of life, which instead begins when the Witness-Position of Consciousness spontaneously Awakens and becomes stable.

In the course of the sixth stage of life, the mechanism of attention, which is the root-action of egoity (felt as separation, self-contraction, or the feeling of relatedness), gradually subsides. In the fullest context of the sixth stage of life, the knot of attention dissolves and all sense of relatedness yields to the Blissful and undifferentiated Feeling of Being. The characteristic Samadhi of the sixth stage of life is Jnana Samadhi, the temporary and exclusive Realization of the Transcendental Self, or Consciousness Itself.

The transition from the sixth stage of life to the seventh stage Realization of Absolute Non-Separateness is the unique Revelation of Avatar Adi Da. Various traditions and individuals previous to Adi Da's Revelation have had sixth stage intuitions or premonitions of the Most Perfect seventh stage Realization, but no one previous to Avatar Adi Da has Realized the seventh stage of life.

The seventh stage Realization is the Gift of Avatar Adi Da to His devotees, Awakened only in the context of the Way of Adidam that He has Revealed and Given. The seventh stage of life begins when His devotee Awakens, by His Grace, from the exclusive Realization of Consciousness to Most Perfect and permanent Identification with Consciousness Itself, Avatar Adi Da's Very (and Inherently Perfect) State. This is Divine Self-Realization, or Divine Enlightenment, the perpetual Samadhi of "Open Eyes" (seventh stage Sahaj Samadhi), in which all "things" are Divinely Recognized without "difference" as merely apparent modifications of the One Self-Existing and Self-Radiant Divine Consciousness. In the course of the seventh stage of life, there may be spontaneous incidents in which psycho-physical states and phenomena do not appear to the notice, being Outshined by the "Bright" Radiance of Consciousness Itself. This Samadhi, which is the ultimate Realization of Divine Existence, culminates in Divine Translation, or the permanent Outshining of all apparent conditions in the Inherently Perfect Radiance and Love-Bliss of the Divine Self-Condition.

In the context of practice of the Way of Adidam, the seven stages of life as Revealed by Avatar Adi Da are not a version of the traditional "ladder" of Spiritual attainment. These stages and their characteristic signs arise naturally in the course of practice for a fully practicing devotee in the Way of Adidam, but the practice itself is oriented to the <u>transcending</u> of the first six stages of life, in the seventh stage Disposition of Inherently Liberated Happiness, Granted by Avatar Adi Da's Grace in His Love-Blissful Spiritual Company.

For Avatar Adi Da's extended Instruction relative to the seven stages of life, see *The Seven Stages Of Life—The Seventeen Companions Of The True Dawn Horse, Book Ten: Transcending The Six Stages Of egoic Life and Realizing The ego-Transcending Seventh Stage Of Life In The Divine Way Of Adidam.*

23. Divine Recognition is the ego-transcending and world-transcending Intelligence of the Divine Self in relation to all conditional phenomena. In the seventh stage of life, the Realizer of the Divine Self simply Abides as Self-Existing and Self-Radiant Consciousness Itself, and he or she Freely Recognizes (or inherently and Most Perfectly comprehends and perceives) all phenomena (including body, mind, conditional self, and conditional world) as transparent (or merely apparent), and un-necessary, and inherently non-binding modifications of the same "Bright" Divine Consciousness.

24. The term "radical" derives from the Latin "radix", meaning "root", and thus it principally means "irreducible", "fundamental", or "relating to the origin". In *The Dawn Horse Testament Of The Ruchira Avatar*, Avatar Adi Da defines "Radical" as "Gone To The Root, Core, Source, or Origin". Because Adi Da Samraj uses "radical" in this literal sense, it appears in quotation marks in His Wisdom-Teaching, in order to distinguish His usage from the common reference to an extreme (often political) view.

25. During the twenty-five years of His Teaching and Revelation Work, Avatar Adi Da elaborately Described every aspect of the practice of Adidam, from the beginning of one's approach to Him to the Most Ultimate Realization of the seventh stage of life.

Avatar Adi Da's Heart-Word is summarized in His twenty-three "Source-Texts". These Texts present, in complete and conclusive detail, His Divine Revelations, Confessions, and Instructions, which are the fruits of His years of Teaching and Revelation Work. In addition to this "Source-Literature", Avatar Adi Da's Heart-Word also includes His "Supportive Texts" (comprising His practical Instruction in all the details of the practice of Adidam, including the fundamental disciplines of diet, health, exercise, sexuality, and the rearing and education of children in a sacred and cooperative community), His "Early Literature" (Written during His Teaching Years), and collections of His Talks.

26. Realization of the inherently Love-Blissful Unity of Divine Consciousness is Given, by Avatar Adi Da's Grace, directly, from the beginning of one's practice of the Way of Adidam—through feeling-Contemplation of Avatar Adi Da's bodily (human) Form, His Spiritual (and Always Blessing) Presence, and His Very (and Inherently Perfect) State. At the same time, the Yoga (or discipline of body, emotion, mind, and breath) whereby that Realization becomes the stable confession and responsibility of each devotee, is a progressive process, unfolding in successive developmental stages of practice and Realization.

27. Ruchira Avatara Bhakti Yoga is the principal Gift, Calling, and Discipline Offered by Adi Da Samraj to all who practice the Way of Adidam.

The phrase "Ruchira Avatara Bhakti Yoga" is itself a summary of the Way of Adidam. "Bhakti", in Sanskrit, is love, adoration, or devotion, while "Yoga" is a Real-God-Realizing discipline or practice. "Ruchira Avatara Bhakti Yoga" is, thus, the Divinely Revealed practice of devotional love for (and response to) the Ruchira Avatar, Adi Da Samraj.

For Avatar Adi Da's essential Instruction in Ruchira Avatara Bhakti Yoga, see also *What, Where, When, How, Why and __Who__ To Remember To Be Happy—The Seventeen Companions Of The True Dawn Horse, Book Thirteen: A Simple Explanation Of The Divine Way Of Adidam (For Children, and __Everyone__ Else)*, Part Three, "Surrender the Faculties of the Body-Mind to Me".

28. An alternate name for Ruchira Avatara Bhakti Yoga (see note 27). Ishta-Guru Bhakti Yoga is the practice ("Yoga") of devotion ("Bhakti") to Avatar Adi Da, the chosen Beloved ("Ishta") Guru of His devotees.

29. This passage is Avatar Adi Da's Revelation of Himself as the Supreme Avatar.

The Ruchira Avatar: In Sanskrit, "Ruchira" means "bright, radiant, effulgent". Thus, the Reference "Ruchira Avatar" indicates that Avatar Adi Da Samraj is the "Bright" (or Radiant) Descent of the Divine Reality Itself (or the Divine Truth Itself, Which Is the Only Real God) into the conditional worlds, Appearing here in bodily (human) Form.

The Da Avatar: "Da" is Sanskrit for "The One Who Gives". Therefore, as the Da Avatar, Adi Da Samraj is the "Bright" Descent of the One and True Divine Giver, the first, last, and only Complete Descent of the Very Divine Person, Who is Named "Da".

The Hridaya Avatar: "Hridaya" is Sanskrit for "the heart". It refers not only to the physical organ but also to the True Heart, the Transcendental (and Inherently Spiritual) Divine Reality. "Hridaya" in combination with "Avatar" signifies that Avatar Adi Da is the Very Incarnation of the Divine Heart Itself, the Divine Incarnation Who Stands in, at, and <u>As</u> the True Heart of every being.

The Love-Ananda Avatar: The Name "Love-Ananda" combines both English ("Love") and Sanskrit ("Ananda", meaning "Bliss"), thus bridging the West and the East, and communicating Avatar Adi Da's Function as the Divine World-Teacher. The combination of "Love" and "Ananda" means "the Divine Love-Bliss". The Name "Love-Ananda" was given to Avatar Adi Da by His principal human Spiritual Master, Swami Muktananda, who spontaneously conferred it upon Avatar Adi Da in 1969. However, Avatar Adi Da did not use the Name "Love-Ananda" until April 1986, after the Great Event that Initiated His Divine "Emergence". As the Love-Ananda Avatar, Adi Da is the Very Incarnation of the Divine Love-Bliss.

The Avabhasa Avatar: The Sanskrit word "Avabhasa" has a rich range of associations. It means "brightness", "appearance", "manifestation", "splendor", "lustre", "light", "knowledge". Its verb root may be interpreted as "shining toward", "shining down", "showing oneself". It is thus synonymous with the English term "the 'Bright'", which Avatar Adi Da has used since His childhood to Describe the Blissfully Self-Luminous Divine Being That He knew even then as the All-Pervading, Transcendental, Inherently Spiritual, and Divine Reality of His own body-mind and of all beings, things, and worlds. As the Avabhasa Avatar, Avatar Adi Da is the Very Incarnation of the Divine Self-"Brightness".

30. Avatar Adi Da Describes His Divine Being on three levels:

This flesh body, this bodily (human) Sign, is My Form, in the sense that it is My Murti, or a kind of Reflection (or Representation) of Me. It is, therefore, a Means for contacting My Spiritual (and Always Blessing) Presence, and, ultimately, My Very (and Inherently Perfect) State.

My Spiritual (and Always Blessing) Presence is Self-Existing and Self-Radiant. It Functions in time and space, and It is also Prior to all time and space.

My Very (and Inherently Perfect) State is always and only utterly Prior to time and space. Therefore, I, As I <u>Am</u> (Ultimately), have no "Function" in time and space. There is no time and space in My Very (and Inherently Perfect) State.

31. *Hridaya Rosary (Four Thorns Of Heart-Instruction)—The Five Books Of The Heart Of The Adidam Revelation, Book Four: The "Late-Time" Avataric Revelation Of The Universally Tangible Divine Spiritual Body, Which Is The Supreme Agent Of The Great Means To Worship and To Realize The True and Spiritual Divine Person (The egoless*

Personal Presence Of Reality and Truth, Which Is The Only Real God) is Avatar Adi Da's summary and exquisitely beautiful Instruction relative to the right, true, full, and fully devotional practice of the Way of Adidam, through which practice Avatar Adi Da's fully practicing devotee Spiritually receives Him with ever greater profundity, and, ultimately (through a process of the Spiritual "melting" of the entire psycho-physical being), Realizes Him most perfectly.

32. There are four different modes, or congregations, of formal approach to Avatar Adi Da Samraj, making it possible for everyone to participate in the Gift of heart-companionship with Him. The total (or full and complete) form of the practice of Adidam is engaged by those in the first and second congregations. Whereas all of Avatar Adi Da's devotees (in all four congregations) engage the fundamental practice of Ruchira Avatara Bhakti Yoga, only members of the first and second congregations are vowed to engage the full range of supportive disciplines (meditation, sacramental worship, guided study, exercise, diet, sexual Yoga, cooperative community living, and so on) Given by Avatar Adi Da Samraj.

For a more detailed description of the four congregations of Avatar Adi Da's devotees, see pp. 184-95.

33. The Ruchira Sannyasin Order is a formal renunciate order composed of uniquely exemplary devotees of Avatar Adi Da Samraj who are practicing in the context of the ultimate stages of life. Avatar Adi Da Samraj is Himself the founding (and senior) Member of the Ruchira Sannyasin Order. The Ruchira Sannyasin Order is the senior cultural authority within the formal gathering of the devotees of Avatar Adi Da Samraj.

34. In Avatar Adi Da's Teaching-Revelation, "Narcissus" is a key symbol of the un-Enlightened individual as a self-obsessed seeker, enamored of his or her own self-image and egoic self-consciousness. In *The Knee Of Listening*, Adi Da Samraj Describes the significance of the archetype of Narcissus:

He is the ancient one visible in the Greek "myth", who was the universally adored child of the gods, who rejected the loved-one and every form of love and relationship, who was finally condemned to the contemplation of his own image, until, as a result of his own act and obstinacy, he suffered the fate of eternal separateness and died in infinite solitude.

35. A Sanskrit word which is traditionally used to refer to the State of being enraptured in a feeling-swoon of Communion with the Divine.

36. See pp. 184-95 for a description of the four congregations of Avatar Adi Da's devotees.

37. Practitioners of the Way of Adidam may at any time Remember or Invoke Avatar Adi Da Samraj (or feel, and thereby Contemplate, His bodily human Form, His Spiritual, and Always Blessing, Presence, and His Very, and Inherently Perfect, State) through simple feeling-Remembrance of Him and by randomly (in daily life and meditation) Invoking Him by Name. (The specific forms of His Names that Avatar Adi Da has Given to be engaged in practice of simple Name-Invocation of Him are listed in chapter three of *The Dawn Horse Testament Of The Ruchira Avatar*.)

   For devotees of Avatar Adi Da Samraj, His Names are the Names of the Very Divine Being. As such, these Names, as Avatar Adi Da Himself has Described, "do not simply <u>mean</u> Real God, or the Blessing of Real God. They are the verbal or audible Form of the Divine." Therefore, Invoking Avatar Adi Da Samraj by Name is a potent and Divinely Empowered form of feeling-Contemplation of Him.

38. Traditionally, devotees have produced artistic images of their Gurus for the purpose of Contemplating the Guru when he or she is either not physically present or (otherwise) no longer physically alive.

   Modern technology makes possible (through photography, videotape, film, holographic imagery, and other means) accurate Representations of the bodily (human) Form of Avatar Adi Da Samraj for devotional use by His formally acknowledged devotees. From the beginning, Avatar Adi Da's devotees are instructed in how to rightly treat and regard the representational Images of Avatar Adi Da in the traditional devotional manner.

39. In the Way of Adidam, meditation is a period of formal devotional Contemplation of Avatar Adi Da Samraj. Meditation is one of the life-disciplines that Avatar Adi Da Samraj has Given to His devotees in the first and second congregations, as a fundamental support for their practice of Ruchira Avatara Bhakti Yoga. For those who have fully adapted to the disciplines of the first and second congregations, the daily practice of meditation includes a period of one and one-half hours in the morning and a period of one hour in the evening. Such daily practice is increased during periods of retreat. Members of the third and fourth congregations may (if they are so moved) engage formal meditation for periods of any length.

40. Avatar Adi Da uses "Perfectly Subjective" to describe the True Divine Source, or "Subject", of the conditional world—as opposed to the conditions, or "objects", of experience. Thus, in the phrase "Perfectly Subjective", the word "Subjective" does not have the sense of

"relating to the merely phenomenal experience, or the arbitrary presumptions, of an individual", but, rather, it has the sense of "relating to Consciousness Itself, the True Subject of all apparent experience".

41. Avatar Adi Da has Described His Blessing to all of His devotees as being made of seven parts, or "Seven Gifts Of Grace". The Seven Gifts are: His Word (Ruchira Avatara Vani), His Sign (Ruchira Avatara Darshan), Devotion to Him (Ruchira Avatara Bhakti), Service to Him (Ruchira Avatara Seva), Discipline in response to Him (Ruchira Avatara Tapas), His Blessing (Ruchira Avatara Kripa), the Blessedness of the relationship with Him (Ruchira Avatara Moksha-Bhava).

Avatar Adi Da Describes these seven Gifts in the Epilogue of *The Dawn Horse Testament Of The Ruchira Avatar.*

42. The Hindi word "Satsang" literally means "true (or right) relationship", "the company of Truth". "Ruchira Avatara Satsang" is the eternal relationship of mutual sacred commitment between Avatar Adi Da Samraj and each true and formally acknowledged practitioner of the Way of Adidam. Once it is consciously assumed by any practitioner, Ruchira Avatara Satsang is an all-inclusive Condition, bringing Divine Grace and Blessings and sacred obligations, responsibilities, and tests into every dimension of the practitioner's life and consciousness.

43. The original, or most basic, <u>functional</u>, <u>practical</u>, and <u>relational disciplines</u> of the Way of Adidam are forms of appropriate human action and responsibility for diet, health, exercise, sexuality, work, service to and support of Avatar Adi Da's Circumstance and Work, and cooperative (formal community) association (or at least significantly participatory affiliation) with other practitioners of the Way of Adidam. The original, or most basic, <u>cultural obligations</u> of the Way of Adidam include meditation, sacramental worship, study of Ruchira Avatar Adi Da's Wisdom-Teaching (and also at least a basic discriminative study of the Great Tradition of religion and Spirituality that is the Wisdom-inheritance of mankind), and regular participation in the "form" (or schedule) of daily, weekly, monthly, and annual devotional activities.

For Avatar Adi Da's detailed Instruction relative to the functional, practical, and relational disciplines and cultural obligations of the Way of Adidam, see *Ruchira Tantra Yoga—The Seventeen Companions Of The True Dawn Horse, Book Nine: The Physical-Spiritual (and Truly Religious) Method Of Mental, Emotional, Sexual, and <u>Whole Bodily Health and Enlightenment</u> In The Divine Way Of Adidam*; *What, Where, When, How, Why, and <u>Who</u> To Remember To Be Happy, Santosha Adidam*; and *The Dawn Horse Testament Of The Ruchira Avatar.*

44. During His physical (human) Lifetime, Avatar Adi Da's devotees go to His Blessing-Seat in order to receive the Gift of directly beholding His bodily (human) Form. After His physical (human) Lifetime, Avatar Adi Da's devotees will behold Him through the Agency of His "Living Murti". Avatar Adi Da Samraj has Instructed that, after His physical (human) Lifetime, there should always be one (and only one) "Living Murti" (or "Murti-Guru") as a Living human Link between Him and His devotees. Each successive "Living Murti" is to be selected from among those members of the Ruchira Sannyasin Order who have been formally acknowledged as Divinely Enlightened devotees of Avatar Adi Da. "Living Murtis" do not function as the independent Guru of practitioners of the Way of Adidam. Rather, they are simply "Representations" of Avatar Adi Da's bodily (human) Form, and a means to Commune with Him.

45. Practitioners of the total (or full and complete) form of the Way of Adidam—in other words, those practitioners who are members of the first and second congregations of Avatar Adi Da's devotees—engage a process which may take (in any individual devotee's case) one of a number of different forms (depending on the qualities of the individual and the intensity of his or her impulse to Realize Reality, or Truth, or Real God) and which unfolds in a sequence of developmental stages. These forms and developmental stages of practice are described in full detail in *The Dawn Horse Testament Of The Ruchira Avatar.*

46. Avatar Adi Da has Empowered three Retreat Sanctuaries as Agents of His Spiritual Transmission. Of these three, the senior Sanctuary is Adidam Samrajashram, the Island of Naitauba in Fiji, where He usually Resides in Perpetual Retreat. It is the place where Avatar Adi Da Himself and the senior renunciate order of the Way of Adidam, the Ruchira Sannyasin Order of the Tantric Renunciates of Adidam, are established. It is the primary Seat of Avatar Adi Da's Divine Blessing Work with the entire Cosmic Mandala.

Avatar Adi Da has Spoken of the significance of this Hermitage Ashram:

AVATAR ADI DA SAMRAJ: Adidam Samrajashram was established so that I might have a Place of Seclusion in which to do My Spiritual Work. This is the Place of My perpetual Samadhi, the Place of My perpetual Self-Radiance. Therefore, this is the Place where people come to participate in My Samadhi and be further Awakened by It. My devotees come to Adidam Samrajashram to magnify their practice of right, true, and full devotion to Me, to practice the Way of Adidam as I Have Revealed and Given It for the sake of most perfectly self-transcending Real-God-Realization.

47. The Mountain Of Attention and Love-Ananda Mahal (formerly known as "Tumomama Sanctuary") were principal sites of Avatar Adi Da's Teaching Demonstration during the years of His Teaching Work. Through His years of Blessing-Infusion of each of these Pilgrimage and Retreat Sanctuaries, He has fully Empowered them for His devotees throughout all time.

48. Residence and daily participation within one of the formally acknowledged communities of Avatar Adi Da's devotees is, as a general rule, a requirement for membership in the first or second congregation.

49. For all members of the first and second congregations of Avatar Adi Da's devotees, the Way of Adidam develops through (potential) developmental stages of practice and Revelation. These stages of practice, and their relationship to the seven stages of life, are Described by Avatar Adi Da Samraj in chapter seventeen of *The Dawn Horse Testament Of The Ruchira Avatar*.

In the phrase "necessary (or, otherwise, potential)", Avatar Adi Da is referring to the fact that His fully practicing devotee <u>must</u> practice in the context of certain of the developmental stages of practice (corresponding to the first three stages of life, the "original" and "basic" contexts of the fourth stage of life, the sixth stage of life, and the seventh stage of life) but may bypass practice in the developmental stages that correspond to "advanced" context of the fourth stage of life and to the fifth stage of life (see note 22).

50. Avatar Adi Da has Given a number of different approaches to the progressive process of Most Perfectly self-transcending Real-God-Realization in the Way of Adidam. In this manner, He accounts for the differences in individuals' qualities—particularly relative to their capability to make use of the various technical practices that support the fundamental practice of Ruchira Avatara Bhakti Yoga and relative to the intensity of their motivation to apply themselves to the Spiritual process in His Company.

Ruchira Avatar Adi Da refers to the most detailed development of the practice of the Way of Adidam as the "technically 'fully elaborated'" form of practice. Each successive stage of practice in the technically "fully elaborated" form of the Way of Adidam is defined by progressively more detailed responsibilities, disciplines, and practices that are assumed in order to take responsibility for the signs of growing maturity in the process of Divine Awakening. A devotee who embraces the technically "fully elaborated" form of practice of the Way of Adidam must (necessarily) be a member of the first congregation of Avatar Adi Da's devotees (in other words, a member of one of the formal renunciate orders—see pp. 185-89). The progress of practice in the technically "fully elaborated" form of the Way of Adidam is monitored, measured, and evaluated by practicing stages (as Described in detail by Avatar Adi Da Samraj in chapter seventeen of *The Dawn Horse Testament Of The Ruchira Avatar*).

Most of Avatar Adi Da's fully practicing devotees will find that they are qualified for a less intensive approach and are moved to a less technical form of the "conscious process" (than is exercised in the technically "fully elaborated" form of the Way of Adidam) and a less intensive and renunciate approach to practice of the Way of Adidam (than is engaged in the first congregation). Thus, most of Avatar Adi Da's fully practicing devotees will take up the technically "simpler" (or even "simplest") form of practice of the Way of Adidam, as members of the second congregation (see pp. 185-89).

In the technically "simpler" practice, Avatar Adi Da's second congregation devotee engages a relatively simple form of technical means of supporting his or her fundamental practice of Ruchira Avatara Bhakti Yoga, and this technical means remains the same throughout the progressive course of developmental stages. In the technically "simplest" practice, Avatar Adi Da's devotee (in either the second or the third or the fourth congregation) engages the fundamental practice of Ruchira Avatara Bhakti Yoga in the simplest possible manner—as "simplest" feeling-Contemplation of Avatar Adi Da, together with the random use of Avatar Adi Da's Principal Name, "Da" (or one of the other Names Which He has Given to be engaged in the practice of simple Name-Invocation of Him).

Avatar Adi Da's fully elaborated Descriptions of the technically "fully elaborated" and the technically "simpler" (or even "simplest") forms of the Way of Adidam are Given in *The Dawn Horse Testament Of The Ruchira Avatar*.

51. Avatar Adi Da has established two formal renunciate orders: The Ruchira Sannyasin Order of the Tantric Renunciates of Adidam (or, simply, the Ruchira Sannyasin Order), and the Avabhasin Lay Renunciate Order of the Tantric Renunciates of Adidam (or, simply, the Lay Renunciate Order).

The senior practicing order in the Way of Adidam is the Ruchira Sannyasin Order. This order is the senior cultural authority within the formal gathering of Avatar Adi Da's devotees. "Sannyasin" is an ancient Sanskrit term for one who has renounced all worldly bonds and who gives himself or herself completely to the Real-God-Realizing or Real-God-Realized life. Members of the Ruchira Sannyasin Order are uniquely exemplary practitioners of the Way of Adidam who are practicing in the context of the advanced (sixth and seventh) stages of life. Members of this Order are legal renunciates and live a life of perpetual retreat. As a general rule, they are to reside at Adidam Samrajashram. The Ruchira Sannyasin Order is the senior authority within the worldwide culture of the devotees of Avatar Adi Da Samraj.

The members of the Ruchira Sannyasin Order have a uniquely significant role among the practitioners of Adidam as Avatar Adi Da's principal human Instruments (or Spiritually mature renunciate devotees) and (in the case of those members who are formally acknowledged as Avatar Adi Da's fully Awakened seventh stage devotees) as the body of practitioners from among whom each of Avatar Adi Da's successive "Living Murtis", or Empowered human Agents, will be selected. Therefore, the Ruchira Sannyasin Order is essential to the perpetual continuation of authentic practice of the Way of Adidam.

The original, principal, and central members of the Ruchira Sannyasin Order are Avatar Adi Da Himself and the Adidama Quandra Mandala. The Adidama Quandra Mandala is comprised of two women devotees, who have for many years practiced most intensively in Avatar Adi Da's most intimate Sphere and have served Him directly in that circumstance.

The Lay Renunciate Order is a cultural service order. It is subordinate to the Ruchira Sannyasin Order and functions within the culture and community of Adidam as an extension of the Ruchira Sannyasin Order. Members of the Lay Renunciate Order provide the inspirational and cultural leadership for the institution, the culture, and the community of Avatar Adi Da's devotees, in service to both the internal sacred devotional culture and the public mission of this worldwide gathering.

The basic responsibility of the Lay Renunciate Order with respect to the gathering of Avatar Adi Da's devotees and the public is to serve them in their fullest possible embrace of the practice of Ruchira Avatara Bhakti Yoga. Members of the Lay Renunciate Order are accountable (for their practice of the Way of Adidam) to the Ruchira Sannyasin Order and to the members of their own order. It is also the responsibility of "lay renunciates" to protect and serve the Ruchira Sannyasin Order, so as to ensure that its members are free to fully engage their life of retreat.

Avatar Adi Da has indicated in *The Dawn Horse Testament Of The Ruchira Avatar* that members of the Lay Renunciate Order who are in practicing stage three (and beyond) function collectively and spontaneously as His Instruments, or means by which His Divine Grace and Awakening Power are Magnified and Transmitted to other devotees and all beings.

52. Avatar Adi Da Samraj uses the term "advanced" to Describe the fourth stage of life (in its "basic" and "advanced" contexts) and the fifth stage of life in the Way of Adidam. He reserves the term "ultimate" to Describe the sixth and seventh stages of life in the Way of Adidam.

53. The "conscious process" is Avatar Adi Da's technical term for those practices through which the mind, or attention, is surrendered and turned about (from egoic self-involvement) to feeling-Contemplation of Him. It is the senior discipline and responsibility of all practitioners in the Way of Adidam. (Avatar Adi Da's Descriptions of the various forms of the "conscious process" are Given in *The Dawn Horse Testament Of The Ruchira Avatar*.)

54. "Conductivity" is Avatar Adi Da's technical term for participation in and responsibility for the movement of natural bodily energies (and, when one is Spiritually Awakened by Him, for the movement of His Spirit-Current of Love-Bliss in Its natural course of association with the body-mind), via intentional exercises of feeling and breathing.

The exercises of Spiritual "conductivity" that Avatar Adi Da Gives to His (formally practicing) Spiritually Awakened devotees are technical whole bodily Yogas of receptive surrender to the Living Spirit-Current. Rudimentary and preparatory technical forms of "conductivity" are Given to beginners in the total practice of the Way of Adidam (and even those who are formally approaching the total practice of the Way of Adidam) in the form of "conscious exercise", and even in the form of all the functional, practical, and relational disciplines whereby body, emotion, mind, and speech are purified, balanced, and energized, or prepared for submission to Avatar Adi Da's Spiritual (and Always Blessing) Presence.

"Conscious exercise" is the discipline of whole bodily feeling-attention and Radiant Happiness—physical, emotional, mental, psychic, total. It is the coordinated exercise of attention, feeling, breath, and body in association with the natural energy of the body-mind, and, as Avatar Adi Da indicates here, potentially with His Spirit-Force. "Conscious exercise" also includes many practical disciplines of posture and breathing and specific exercise routines to be engaged in daily practice in the Way of Adidam.

55. "Hearing" is a technical term used by Avatar Adi Da to Describe most fundamental understanding of the act of egoity (or self-contraction). Hearing is the unique capability to directly transcend the self-contraction, such that, simultaneous with that transcendence, there is the intuitive awakening to the Revelation of the Divine Person and Self-Condition. The capability of true hearing can only be Granted by

Avatar Adi Da's Grace, to His fully practicing devotee who has effectively completed the process of listening. Only on the basis of such hearing can Spiritually Awakened practice of the Way of Adidam truly (or with full responsibility) begin.

I Am Heard When My Listening Devotee Has Truly (and Thoroughly) Observed the ego-"I" and Understood it (Directly, In the moments Of self-Observation, and Most Fundamentally, or In its Totality).

I Am Heard When the ego-"I" Is Altogether (and Thoroughly) Observed and (Most Fundamentally) Understood, Both In The Tendency To Dissociate and In The Tendency To Become Attached (or To Cling By Wanting Need, or To Identify With others, and things, and circumstances egoically, and Thus To Dramatize The Seeker, Bereft Of Basic Equanimity, Wholeness, and The Free Capability For Simple Relatedness).

I Am Heard When the ego-"I" Is Thoroughly (and Most Fundamentally) Understood To Be Contraction-Only, An Un-Necessary and Destructive Motive and Design, Un-Naturally and Chronically Added To Cosmic Nature and To all relations, and An Imaginary Heart-Disease (Made To Seem Real, By Heart-Reaction).

I Am Heard When This Most Fundamental Understanding Of The Habit Of "Narcissus" Becomes The Directly Obvious Realization Of The Heart, Radiating Beyond Its Own (Apparent) Contraction.

I Am Heard When The Beginning Is Full, and The Beginning Is Full (and Ended) When Every Gesture Of self-Contraction (In The Context Of The First Three Stages Of Life, and Relative To Each and All Of The Principal Faculties, Of body, emotion, mind, and breath) Is (As A Rather Consistently Applied and humanly Effective Discipline) Observed (By Natural feeling-perception), Tacitly (and Most Fundamentally) Understood, and Really (Directly and Effectively) Felt Beyond (In The Prior Feeling Of Unqualified Relatedness). (The Dawn Horse Testament Of The Ruchira Avatar, chapter nineteen)

When, in the practice of the Way of Adidam, hearing (or most fundamental self-understanding) is steadily exercised in meditation and in life, the native feeling of the heart ceases to be chronically constricted by self-contraction. The heart then begins to Radiate as love in response to the Spiritual (and Always Blessing) Presence of Avatar Adi Da.

This emotional and Spiritual response of the whole being is what Avatar Adi Da calls "seeing". Seeing is emotional conversion from the reactive emotions that characterize egoic self-obsession, to the open-hearted, Radiant Happiness that characterizes God-Love and Spiritual devotion to Avatar Adi Da. This true and stable emotional conversion coincides with true and stable receptivity to Avatar Adi

Da's Spiritual Transmission, and both of these are prerequisites to further Spiritual advancement in the Way of Adidam.

Seeing Is self-Transcending Participation In <u>What</u> (and <u>Who</u>) <u>Is</u>. Seeing Is Love. Seeing, or Love, Is Able (By My Grace) To "Locate", Recognize, and Feel My All-Pervading Spiritual Radiance (and My Spirit-Identity, <u>As</u> The Divine Person, or The "Bright" and Only One <u>Who</u> <u>Is</u>). Therefore, Seeing Is Heart-Felt and Whole bodily Identification Of The Love-Bliss-Presence and Person (or Mere Being) Of The Divine. Seeing Is Spiritually Activated Conversion Of attention, emotion, and the Total psycho-physical personality From self-Contraction To The Spiritual Form (or Tangible Spiritual Presence) Of Real God (or The Necessarily Divine Reality and Truth, Itself), and This Via My Spirit-Baptism (or Divine and Inherently Perfect Hridaya-Shaktipat, or Divine and Inherently Perfect Heart-Awakening, and The Subsequent Apparent Descent and Circulation Of The Divine Spirit-Force Into and Through and, Ultimately, Beyond the body-mind Of My Progressively Awakening Devotee). Seeing Is Spontaneous (or Heart-Moved) Devotional Sacrifice Of the self-Contraction. Seeing Is The "Radical" (or Directly self-Transcending) Reorientation Of conditional Existence To The Transcendental, Inherently Spiritual, and Inherently Perfect Divine Self-Condition (and Source-Condition) In Whom (or In Which) conditional self and conditional worlds Apparently arise and Always Already Inhere.

Seeing, Like Hearing, Is A "Radical" (or "Gone To The Root, Core, Source, or Origin") Capability That Can and Should Be Exercised moment to moment. When There Is (In any moment) Real Seeing Of Me, There Is The Capability To Contact Me Spiritually and Enter Into Communion With Me Spiritually. When You Have Awakened (By My Grace) To See Me Truly, Then The Act (and Sadhana) Of Contacting Me Spiritually Does Not, In <u>every</u> moment Of Its Exercise, Require That You Come Into The Physical Sphere Of My Bodily (Human) Form (or, After The Physical Lifetime Of My Bodily Human Form, Into The physical Sphere Of My "Living Murti") or That You Enter Into a place Spiritually Empowered By Me. My Devotee Who Sees Me Is (In The General Course Of moment to moment Practice Of Devotion To Me) Capable Of Contacting Me Spiritually In any circumstance, By Using The "Radical" Virtue Of Hearing and Seeing To Go Beyond The self-Contracting Tendency.

Seeing Is Simply Attraction To Me, and Feeling Me, As My Spiritual (and Always Blessing) Presence, and This Most Fundamentally, At The Root, Core, Source, or Origin Of The Emergence Of My Presence "here" (At and In Front Of The Heart, or At and In The Root-Context Of the body-mind, or At and In The Source-Position, and, Ultimately, As The Source-Condition, Of conditional, or psycho-physical, Existence Itself).

Seeing Is Knowing Me As My Spiritual (and Always Blessing) Presence, Just As Tangibly, and With The Same Degree Of Clarity, As You Would Differentiate The Physical Appearance Of My Bodily (Human) Form From the physical appearance of the bodily (human) form of any other.

To See Me Is A Clear and "Radical" Knowledge Of Me, About Which There Is No Doubt. To See Me Is A Sudden, Tacit Awareness, Like Walking Into a "thicker" air or atmosphere, or Suddenly Feeling a breeze, or Jumping Into water and Noticing The Difference In Density Between the air and the water. This Tangible Feeling Of Me Is (In any particular moment) Not Necessarily (Otherwise) Associated With effects in the body-mind . . . , but It Is, Nevertheless, Felt At The Heart and Even All Over the body.

Seeing Me Is One-Pointedness In The "Radical" Conscious Process Of Heart-Devotion To Me. (The Dawn Horse Testament Of The Ruchira Avatar, chapter twenty)

For Avatar Adi Da's fundamental Instruction relative to hearing and seeing, see chapters nineteen and twenty of *The Dawn Horse Testament Of The Ruchira Avatar*, or chapters twenty-one through twenty-three and chapters twenty-four through twenty-eight of *The Heart Of The Dawn Horse Testament Of The Ruchira Avatar Of The Ruchira Avatar*.

56. "Listening" is Avatar Adi Da's term for the orientation, disposition, and beginning practice of the Way of Adidam. A listening devotee "listens" to Avatar Adi Da Samraj by "considering" His Teaching Argument and His Leelas, and by practicing feeling-Contemplation of Him (primarily of His bodily human Form). In the total (or full and complete) practice of the Way of Adidam, effective listening is the necessary prerequisite for true hearing and true seeing (see note 55).

For Avatar Adi Da's fundamental Instruction relative to the listening process, see chapter nineteen of *The Dawn Horse Testament Of The Ruchira Avatar*, or chapters twenty-one through twenty-three of *The Heart Of The Dawn Horse Testament Of The Ruchira Avatar*.

57. The Sansrit word "Samadhi" is traditionally used to denote various exalted states that appear in the context of esoteric meditation and Realization. The Samadhi to which Avatar Adi Da refers here, however, is the Samadhi of the seventh (or Divinely Enlightened) stage of life, which Samadhi is Revealed and Given only by Avatar Adi Da Samraj.

Perfect Samadhi, or seventh stage Sahaj Samadhi, is the unqualified Realization of Reality, or Truth, or Real God—the eternal, inherent (or native), and, thus, truly "Natural" ("Sahaj"), State of Unconditional Divine Self-Consciousness, free of dependence on any form of meditation, effort, discipline, experience, or conditional knowledge. It is the "Open-Eyed" Realization of the Formless Ecstasy of Divine Existence, the Realization of Absolute Non-Separateness, free of the binding (or limiting) power of attention, the body-mind, and all arising conditions.

For Avatar Adi Da's extended Instruction relative to seventh stage Sahaj Samadhi, see *The All-Completing and Final Divine Revelation To Mankind.*

58. "Darshan", in Hindi, literally means "seeing", "sight of", or "vision of". To receive Darshan of Avatar Adi Da is, most fundamentally, to behold His bodily (human) Form (either by being in His physical Company or by seeing a photograph or other visual representation of Him), and (thereby) to receive the spontaneous Blessing He Grants Freely whenever His bodily (human) Form is beheld in the devotional manner. In the Way of Adidam, Darshan of Avatar Adi Da is the very essence of the practice, and one of the most potent forms of receiving Avatar Adi Da's Blessing is to participate in the formal occasions of Darshan—during which Avatar Adi Da Samraj Sits silently in the company of His devotees, often gazing at each individual one by one—to which His devotees who are on retreat in His Company (or who, otherwise, reside and serve in His physical Company) may be invited.

By extension, "Darshan" of Avatar Adi Da Samraj may refer to any means by which His Blessing-Influence is felt and received—including His Written or Spoken Word, photographs or videotapes of His bodily (human) Form, recordings of His Voice, Leelas (or Stories) of His Teaching and Blessing Work, places or objects He has Spiritually Empowered, visualization of His bodily (human) Form in the mind, and simple, heart-felt Remembrance of Him.

59. "Seva" is Sanskrit for "service". Thus, "Ruchira Avatara Seva" is "service to the Ruchira Avatar, Adi Da Samraj".

Service to one's Spiritual Master, or Guru, is traditionally treasured as one of the great Means of Spiritual Realization. In the Way of Adidam, each practitioner finds many specific ways to serve Avatar Adi Da Samraj and His Divine Work of world-Blessing. In the largest sense, to serve Avatar Adi Da constantly is to live every action and, indeed, one's entire life, as direct heart-Communion with and responsive obedience and conformity to Avatar Adi Da in every possible and appropriate way.

60. "Tapas" is Sanskrit for "heat", or, by extension, "self-discipline engaged as part of the religious and Spiritual process". (The "heat" of self-discipline is traditionally understood as one of the primary means of purifying the psycho-physical being.) Thus, "Ruchira Avatara

Tapas" means "the self-discipline Given by the Ruchira Avatar, Adi Da Samraj, to His formally acknowledged devotees".

61. Avatar Adi Da Samraj is the Divine World-Teacher because His Wisdom-Teaching is the uniquely Perfect Instruction to every being—in this (and every) world—in the total process of Divine Enlightenment. Furthermore, Avatar Adi Da Samraj constantly Extends His Regard to the entire world (and the entire Cosmic domain)—not on the political or social level, but as a Spiritual matter, constantly Working to Bless and Purify all beings everywhere.

62. "Hridayam" is Sanskrit for "heart". It refers not only to the physical organ but also to the True Heart, the Transcendental (and Inherently Spiritual) Divine Person and Presence That Is the Native Reality of all and All. "Da Hridayam" is one of Avatar Adi Da's Divine Names, signifying that He Stands in, at, and As the True Heart of every being.

63. Avatar Adi Da's Name "Avabhasa" is a Sanskrit word associated with a variety of meanings: "brightness", "appearance", "splendor", "lustre", "light", "knowledge". It is thus synonymous with the English term "the 'Bright'", which Avatar Adi Da has used since His Illumined boyhood to Describe the Blissfully Self-Luminous Divine Being, eternally, infinitely, and inherently Self-Radiant, Which He knew even then as the All-Pervading, Transcendental, Inherently Spiritual, and Divine Reality of His own body-mind and of all beings, things, and worlds.

64. "Santosha" is Sanskrit for "satisfaction" or "contentment"—qualities associated with a sense of completion. These qualities are characteristic of no-seeking, the fundamental Principle of Avatar Adi Da's Wisdom-Teaching and of His entire Revelation of Truth. As Santosha Da, Avatar Adi Da Samraj is the Divine Giver of Perfect Divine Contentedness, or Perfect Searchlessness.

Epilogue

65. With the phrase "may (or, otherwise, must) occur", Avatar Adi Da points to the fact that, in the case of all of His first-congregation and second-congregation devotees, the progressive process of the Way of Adidam must (necessarily) include practice in the "original" context and the "basic" context of the fourth stage of life, and it must (necessarily) include practice in the context of the sixth stage of life, but it may or may not include practice in the "advanced" context of the fourth stage of life and in the context of the fifth stage of life. Only those practitioners of the Way of Adidam who exhibit unusually strong subtle tendencies of mind may need to fulfill the Yoga of Spir-

itual ascent in the "advanced" context of the fourth stage of life, and perhaps also in the fifth stage of life. (See note 22.)

For Avatar Adi Da's extended Instruction relative to the stages of life (including the "original", "basic", and "advanced" contexts of the fourth stage of life), see *The Seven Stages Of Life—The Seventeen Companions Of The True Dawn Horse, Book Ten: Transcending The Six Stages Of egoic Life and Realizing The ego-Transcending Seventh Stage Of Life In The Divine Way Of Adidam*. For Avatar Adi Da's discussion of the early transition to the sixth stage of life, see *The Dawn Horse Testament Of The Ruchira Avatar* (chapter forty-three) and *Santosha Adidam* (Part One, section II).

66. Conventionally, "self-possessed" means possessed of oneself—or in full control (calmness, or composure) of one's feelings, impulses, habits, and actions. Avatar Adi Da uses the term to indicate the state of being possessed by one's egoic self, or controlled by chronically self-referring (or egoic) tendencies of attention, feeling, thought, desire, and action.

What You Can Do Next

Contact one of our centers.

■ Sign up for our preliminary course, "The <u>Only</u> Truth That Sets The Heart Free". This course will prepare you to become a fully practicing devotee of Avatar Adi Da Samraj.

■ Or sign up for any of our other classes, seminars, events, or retreats, or for a study course available by correspondence:

AMERICAS
12040 North Seigler Road
Middletown, CA 95461
(800) 524-4941
(707) 928-4936

PACIFIC-ASIA
12 Seibel Road
Henderson
Auckland 1008
New Zealand
64-9-838-9114

AUSTRALIA
P.O. Box 460
Roseville, NSW 2069
Australia
61-2-9416-7951

EUROPE-AFRICA
Annendaalderweg 10
6105 AT Maria Hoop
The Netherlands
31 (0)20 468 1442

THE UNITED KINGDOM
London, England
0181-7317550

E-MAIL: correspondence@adidam.org

Read these books by and about the Divine World-Teacher, Ruchira Avatar Adi Da Samraj:

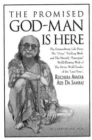

■ *The Promised God-Man Is Here*
The Extraordinary Life-Story, The "Crazy" Teaching-Work, and The Divinely "Emerging" World-Blessing Work Of The Divine World-Teacher Of The "Late-Time", Ruchira Avatar Adi Da Samraj, by Carolyn Lee, Ph.D.—the profound, heart-rending, humorous, miraculous, wild—and true—story of the Divine Person Alive in human Form. Essential reading as background for the study of Avatar Adi Da's books.

■ *See My Brightness Face to Face*
A Celebration of the Ruchira Avatar, Adi Da Samraj, and the First Twenty-Five Years of His Divine Revelation Work—a magnificent year-by-year pictorial celebration of Ruchira Avatar Adi Da's Divine Work with His devotees, from 1972-1997. Includes a wealth of selections from His Talks and Writings, numerous Stories of His Divine Work told by His devotees, and over 100 color photographs.

■ *Aham Da Asmi (Beloved, I Am Da)*
The Five Books Of The Heart Of The Adidam Revelation, Book One: The "Late-Time" Avataric Revelation Of The True and Spiritual Divine Person (The egoless Personal Presence Of Reality and Truth, Which Is The Only Real God)
This Ecstatic Scripture, the first of His twenty-three "Source-Texts", contains Ruchira Avatar Adi Da's magnificent Confession of His Identity as the Very Divine Person and Source-Condition of all and All.

After reading *Aham Da Asmi*, continue your reading with the remaining books of *The Five Books Of The Heart Of The Adidam Revelation* (the *Ruchira Avatara Gita*, *Hridaya Rosary*, and *Eleutherios*). Then you will be ready to go on to *The Seventeen Companions Of The True Dawn Horse* (see pp. 207-211). These and other books by and about Ruchira Avatar Adi Da Samraj can be ordered directly from the Dawn Horse Press by calling:

(800) 524-4941 (from within North America)
(707) 928-4936 (from outside North America)

or by writing to:

The Dawn Horse Press
12040 North Seigler Road
Middletown, CA 95461

Or you can order these, or any of the other products distributed by the Dawn Horse Press, by visiting the Dawn Horse Press on-line at: **http://dhp.adidam.org**.

Visit our website:
http://www.adidam.org.

Our award-winning website contains a wealth of photographs of Ruchira Avatar Adi Da Samraj, audio-clips of Him Speaking, excerpts from His Writings, and recent Stories of His world-Blessing Work. The website also has a full listing of Adidam regional centers worldwide.

For a full description of all the forms of involvement in the Way of Adidam, see "Surely Come to Me" on pp. 183-203.

RUCHIRA AVATAR ADI DA SAMRAJ
Adidam Samrajashram (Naitauba), Fiji, 1997

"Surely Come to Me"

An Invitation to the Way of Adidam

I __Am__ The Divine Heart-Master. I Take My Stand In The Heart Of My Devotee. Have You Realized The Heart, Who __Is__ The Mystery Of You and Me?

How Could I Deny Heart-Vision To My Loved-One?
How Could I Delay The Course Of My Beloved?

Like An Intimate Family Servant, I Dearly Serve My Devotee.

Like A Wealthy Friend, I Freely Give To My Devotee.

Like A Mad Priest, I Even Worship My Devotee, With Love Itself.

Like An Innocent Boy At First Love, I Would Awaken My Devotee In Radiant Chambers.

Where The Wound Of Love Churns and Never Heals, I Wait, Longing To Celebrate The Brilliant Sight Of My Devotee.

Come Slowly or Quickly, but Surely Come To Me.

Touch My Heart, and I Will Widen You To God-Knows-Where.

THE DAWN HORSE TESTAMENT OF THE RUCHIRA AVATAR

You are Blessed to be alive at the time of the Greatest of Revelations—the All-Completing Revelation of Real God promised by all the religious and Spiritual traditions of mankind. The Divine World-Teacher, Ruchira Avatar Adi Da Samraj, is that All-Completing Revelation. He is the Perfect Fulfillment of that universal promise.

Ruchira Avatar Adi Da Samraj Offers you a devotional relationship which literally brings His tangible Divine Blessing into your life. For the sake of all who are moved to go beyond all the dead-ends of ordinary life and all the dead-ends of Spiritual seeking, Ruchira Avatar Adi Da

Samraj has Revealed and Given the unique Way of Adidam—the only complete Way to Realize the True and Spiritual Divine Person, Who Is Reality Itself, or Truth Itself, or Real God.

You have before you now the greatest of life-choices: How are you going to respond to the Most Perfect Revelation of Real God?

How To Respond

The Divine World-Teacher, Ruchira Avatar Adi Da Samraj, Calls you to formally become His devotee—which means to formally take up practice of the Way of Adidam, the Divinely Enlightening Way of life He has Revealed and Given for the sake of all beings.

Because those who approach Him have different heart-needs and different life-circumstances to account for, Ruchira Avatar Adi Da has created four congregations of formal approach to Him. These four congregations, together, make up the Eleutherian Pan-Communion of Adidam (or, simply, the Adidam Pan-Communion). Which of the four congregations of the Adidam Pan-Communion you should apply to for membership depends on the strength of your impulse to respond to Avatar Adi Da's Revelation and on your life-circumstance.

Take Up the Total Practice
of the Way of Adidam

*(The First and Second Congregations
of the Adidam Pan-Communion)*

The first and second congregations of the Adidam Pan-Communion are for practitioners of the <u>total</u> practice of the Way of Adidam (and for student-novices, who are formally approaching the total practice of the Way of Adidam). In particular, the first congregation is for those who have dedicated their lives <u>one-pointedly</u> to Realizing Real God—it is the congregation made up of the two formal renunciate orders of Adidam: the Ruchira Sannyasin Order of the Tantric Renunciates of Adidam, and the Avabhasin Lay Renunciate Order of the Tantric Renunciates of Adidam. The second congregation is made up of student-novices, student-beginners, and members of the Lay Congregationist Order of Adidam (which is the general lay practicing and serving order of Ruchira Avatar Adi Da's lay devotees who have advanced beyond the student-beginner stage).

To take up the total practice of the Way of Adidam is to take full advantage of the opportunity Offered by Ruchira Avatar Adi Da Samraj—it is to enter fully into the Process of Real-God-Realization. That Process of Real-God-Realization is a unique ordeal, which necessarily requires application to a wide range of functional, practical, relational, and cultural self-disciplines Revealed and Given by Ruchira Avatar Adi Da Samraj for the sake of that Divine Process. These disciplines allow the body-mind to be made ever more available to Ruchira Avatar Adi Da's Blessing Transmission. They range from foundation practices relative to diet, health, sexuality, and work, to the core devotional practices of meditation, sacramental worship, and study of Avatar Adi Da's Wisdom-Teaching. The Way of Adidam is not a "talking" school based on merely adhering to a certain philosophy or upholding a certain religious point of view. Rather, the Way of Adidam is a "practicing" school, in which you participate in the Process of Real-God-Realization with every aspect of your being.

If you want to enter fully into the Process of Real-God-Realization in the Company of Ruchira Avatar Adi Da Samraj, then you should apply to become a member of the second congregation of the Adidam Pan-Communion—and if you are moved to <u>one-pointedly</u> dedicate your life to the Process of Real-God-Realization, after a period of exemplary practice in the second congregation, you may apply to practice as a formal renunciate in the first congregation. (The life of members of the first and second congregations is described and pictured on pp. 196-200.)

When you apply for membership in the second congregation of the Adidam Pan-Communion (the first step for all who want to take up the total practice of the Way of Adidam), you will be asked to prepare yourself by taking "The <u>Only</u> Truth That Sets the Heart Free", a course of formal study and "consideration" (lasting four to six weeks), in which you examine the Opportunity Offered to you by Avatar Adi Da Samraj, and learn what it means to embrace the total practice of the Way of Adidam as a second-congregation devotee of Ruchira Avatar Adi Da. (To register for this preparatory course, please contact the regional or territorial center nearest to you [see p. 203], or e-mail us at: correspondence@adidam.org.) After completing this period of study, you may formally enter the second congregation by becoming a student-novice.

Entering any of the four congregations of Adidam involves taking a formal vow of devotion and service to Avatar Adi Da Samraj. This vow is a profound—and, indeed, eternal—commitment. You take this vow (for whichever congregation you are entering) when you are certain that your great and true heart-impulse is to be devoted, forever, to Avatar Adi Da Samraj as your Divine Heart-Master. If you recognize Avatar Adi Da as the Living

Divine Person—your Perfect Guide and Help and your eternal and most intimate Heart-Companion—then you know that this vow is a priceless Gift, and you joyfully embrace the great responsibility it represents.

As a student-novice (formally approaching the total practice of the Way of Adidam), you are initiated into formal meditation and sacramental worship, you begin to adapt to a wide range of life-disciplines, and you begin to participate in the life of the cooperative community of Ruchira Avatar Adi Da's devotees. As a student-novice, you engage in an intensive period of study and "consideration" of the Way of Adidam in all of its details. And, as your practice matures, you are given more and more access to the cultural life of the formally acknowledged practitioners of the total practice of Adidam. After a minimum of three to six months of practice as a student-novice, you may apply for formal acknowledgement as a fully practicing member of the second congregation.

If you find that you are steadily and profoundly moved to dedicate your life <u>one-pointedly</u> to Ruchira Avatar Adi Da Samraj and the Process of Real-God-Realization in His Spiritual Company, then, after a demonstration period of exemplary practice as a member of the second congregation, you may apply to practice as a formal renunciate in the first congregation of the Adidam Pan-Communion.

The two formal renunciate orders in the Way of Adidam are the Lay Renunciate Order and the Ruchira Sannyasin Order. The senior of the two orders is the Ruchira Sannyasin Order, which is the senior cultural authority within the gathering of all four congregations of Avatar Adi Da's devotees. The members of the Ruchira Sannyasin Order are the most exemplary formal renunciate practitioners practicing in the ultimate (sixth and seventh) stages of life in the Way of Adidam. The core of the Ruchira Sannyasin Order, and its senior governing members, will, in the future, be those devotees who have Realized Divine Enlightenment. Ruchira Avatar Adi Da Samraj Himself is

the Founding Member of the Ruchira Sannyasin Order, and will, throughout His Lifetime, remain its Senior Member in every respect.

The Ruchira Sannyasin Order is a retreat Order, whose members are legal renunciates. They are supported and protected in their unique Spiritual role by the Lay Renunciate Order, which is a cultural service Order that serves an inspirational and aligning role for all devotees of Avatar Adi Da.

First-congregation devotees have a special role to play in the Way of Adidam. Adi Da Samraj must have unique human Instrumentality—Spiritually Awakened and Divinely Self-Realized devotees—through whom He can continue to do His Divine Transmission Work after His physical Lifetime. No human being, not even one of Avatar Adi Da's Divinely Enlightened devotees, can "succeed" Ruchira Avatar Adi Da Samraj, in the way that, traditionally, a senior devotee often succeeds his or her Spiritual Master.* Avatar Adi Da Samraj is the Complete Incarnation of the Divine Person—He is truly the Completion of all Spiritual lineages in all times and places. Thus, He remains forever the Divine Awakener and Liberator of all beings. His Spiritually Awakened renunciate devotees will collectively function as His Spiritual Instruments, allowing His Blessing-Power to Pervade and Influence the world.

To become a fully practicing devotee of Avatar Adi Da Samraj (in the second congregation, and potentially moving on to the first congregation), call or write one of our regional centers (see p. 203) and sign up for our preliminary course, "The Only Truth That Sets the Heart Free".

*Adi Da Samraj has Said that, after His physical (human) Lifetime, there should always be one (and only one) "Murti-Guru" as a Living Link between Him and His devotees. Each successive "Murti-Guru" is to be selected from among those members of the Ruchira Sannyasin Order who have been formally acknowledged as Divinely Enlightened devotees of Adi Da. "Murti-Gurus" do not function as the independent Guru of practitioners of the Way of Adidam. Rather, they are simply Representations of Adi Da's bodily (human) Form, and a means to Commune with Him.

The Adidam Youth Fellowship

Young people (25 and under) are also offered a special form of relationship to Avatar Adi Da—the Adidam Youth Fellowship. The Adidam Youth Fellowship has two membership bodies—friends and practicing members. A friend of the Adidam Youth Fellowship is simply invited into a culture of other young people who want to learn more about Avatar Adi Da Samraj and His Happiness-Realizing Way of Adidam. A formally practicing member of the Adidam Youth Fellowship acknowledges that he or she has found his or her True Heart-Friend and Master in the Person of Avatar Adi Da Samraj, and wishes to enter into a direct, self-surrendering Spiritual relationship with Him as the Means to True Happiness. Practicing members of the Youth Fellowship embrace a series of disciplines that are similar to (but simpler than) the practices engaged by adult members of the second congregation of Adidam. Both friends and members are invited to special retreat events from time to time, where they can associate with other young devotees of Avatar Adi Da.

To become a member of the Adidam Youth Fellowship, or to learn more about this form of relationship to Avatar Adi Da, call or write:

Vision of Mulund Institute (VMI)
10336 Loch Lomond Road, Suite 146
Middletown, CA 95461
PHONE: (707) 928-6932
FAX: (707) 928-5619
E-MAIL: vmi@adidam.org

Become an Advocate of the Way of Adidam

(In the Fourth Congregation of the Adidam Pan-Communion)

The fourth congregation of the Adidam Pan-Communion is for those who are attracted to the life of devotional intimacy with Avatar Adi Da Samraj and are moved to serve His world-Blessing Work, but who are not presently moved or able to take up the full range of disciplines required of members of the first and second congregations. Thus, if you embrace the fourth-congregation practice, you receive Avatar Adi Da's Spiritual Blessings in your life by assuming the most basic level of responsibility as His devotee. The fourth-congregation practice allows you to develop and deepen true devotional intimacy with Avatar Adi Da, but, because it does not involve the full range of disciplines, it always remains a beginning form of the practice of Adidam. If, as a member of the fourth congregation, you are eventually moved to advance beyond the beginning, you are always invited to transition to the second congregation and embrace the total—and, potentially, Divinely Enlightening—practice of the Way of Adidam.

A principal organization within the fourth congregation is the Transnational Society of Advocates of the Adidam Revelation. Advocates are individuals who recognize Ruchira Avatar Adi Da Samraj as a Source of Wisdom and Blessing in their own lives and for the world, and who want to make a practical response. Advocates serve Ruchira Avatar Adi Da's world-Blessing Work by actively serving the dissemination of His Wisdom-Teaching and by actively advocating Him and the Way of Adidam.

When you become an advocate, you make a formal vow of devotion and service to Ruchira Avatar Adi Da Samraj. As described on pp. 186-87, this vow is a profound and eternal commitment to Avatar Adi Da as Your Divine Heart-Master. By taking this vow, you are committing yourself to perform a specific consistent service to Avatar Adi Da and His Blessing Work, and to embrace the fundamental devotional practice that Avatar Adi Da Gives to all His devotees. This is the practice of Ruchira Avatara Bhakti Yoga—devotion to Ruchira Avatar Adi Da Samraj as your Divine Heart-Master. Advocates do the simplest form of this great practice, which Ruchira Avatar Adi Da summarizes as "Invoke Me, Feel Me, Breathe Me, Serve Me".

The advocate vow is also a commitment to make a monthly donation to help support the publication of Avatar Adi Da's supremely precious Wisdom-Literature (as well as publications about Him and the Way of Adidam), as well as paying an annual membership fee that supports the services of the Society of Advocates.

In addition, Advocates offer their services in the form of whatever practical or professional skills they can bring to creatively serve Ruchira Avatar Adi Da and the Way of Adidam.

To become a member of the Transnational Society of Advocates of the Adidam Revelation, call or write one of our regional centers (see p. 203), or e-mail us at:

correspondence@adidam.org

In addition to members of the Transnational Society of Advocates, those who live in traditional cultures around the world are invited to practice as members of the fourth congregation. The opportunity to practice in the fourth congregation is also extended to all those who, because of physical or other functional limitations, are unable to take up the total practice of the Way of Adidam as required in the first and second congregations.

To become a member of the fourth congregation of Adidam, call or write one of our regional centers (see p. 203), or e-mail us at: correspondence@adidam.org.

Serve the Divine World-Teacher
and His World-Blessing Work
via Patronage or Unique Influence

(The Third Congregation
of the Adidam Pan-Communion)

We live at a time when the destiny of mankind and of even the planet itself hangs desperately in the balance. The Divine World-Teacher, Ruchira Avatar Adi Da Samraj, has Manifested at this precarious moment in history in order to Reveal the Way of true Liberation from the disease of egoity. It is only That Gift of true Liberation that can reverse the disastrous trends of our time.

It is the sacred responsibility of those who respond to Ruchira Avatar Adi Da to provide the means for His Divine Work to achieve truly great effect in the world. He must be given the practical means to Bless all beings and to Work with His devotees and others responding to Him in all parts of the world, in whatever manner He is spontaneously moved to do so. He must be able to move freely from one part of the world to another. He must be able to establish Hermitages in various parts of the world, where He can Do His silent Work of Blessing, and where He can also Work with His devotees and others who can be of significant help in furthering His Work by receiving them into His physical Company. Ruchira Avatar Adi Da must also be able to gather around Him His most exemplary formal renunciate devotees—and such formal renunciates must be given practical support so that they can be entirely and one-pointedly devoted to serving Ruchira Avatar Adi Da and to living the life of perpetual Spiritual retreat in His physical Company. And the mere fact that Real God is Present in the world must become as widely known as possible, both through the publication and dissemination of books by and about Ruchira Avatar Adi Da and through public advocacy by people of influence.

If you are a man or woman of unique wealth or unique influence in the world, we invite you to serve Ruchira Avatar Adi Da's world-Blessing Work by becoming His patron. Truly, patronage of the Divine World-Teacher, Ruchira Avatar Adi Da Samraj, exceeds all other possible forms of philanthropy. You are literally helping to change the destiny of countless people by helping to support Ruchira Avatar Adi Da in His world-Blessing Work. You make it possible for Ruchira Avatar Adi Da's Divine Influence to reach people who might otherwise never come to know of Him. You make it possible for Him to make fullest use of His own physical Lifetime—the unique bodily Lifetime of Real God, Perfectly Incarnate. To make the choice to serve Avatar Adi Da via your patronage or unique influence is to allow your own life and destiny, and the life and destiny of all of mankind, to be transformed in the most Graceful way possible.

As a member of the third congregation, your relationship to Ruchira Avatar Adi Da is founded on a vow of Ruchira Avatara Bhakti Yoga—a vow of devotion, through which you commit yourself to serve His Work. In the course of your service to Ruchira Avatar Adi Da (and in daily life altogether), you live your vow of devotion by invoking Him, feeling Him, breathing Him, and serving Him (without being expected to engage the full range of disciplines practiced in the first two congregations). At all times, this practice is the means Ruchira Avatar Adi Da has Given for His third-congregation devotees to remain connected to His constant Blessing. In addition, Ruchira Avatar Adi Da has invited, and may continue to invite, members of the third congregation into His physical Company to receive His Divine Blessing.

If you are able to serve Avatar Adi Da Samraj in this crucial way, please contact us at:

Third Congregation Advocacy
12040 North Seigler Road
Middletown, CA 95461
phone number: (707) 928-4800
FAX: (707) 928-4618
e-mail: third_congregation@adidam.org

The Life of a Formally Practicing Devotee of Ruchira Avatar Adi Da Samraj

(in the First or Second Congregation of Adidam)

Everything you do as a devotee of Ruchira Avatar Adi Da Samraj in the first congregation or the second congregation of Adidam is an expression of your heart-response to Him as your Divine Heart-Master. The life of cultivating that response is Ruchira Avatara Bhakti Yoga—or the Real-God-Realizing practice ("Yoga") of devotion ("Bhakti") to the Ruchira Avatar, Adi Da Samraj.

The great practice of Ruchira Avatara Bhakti Yoga necessarily transforms the whole of your life. Every function, every relationship, every action is moved by the impulse of devotional heart-surrender to Adi Da Samraj.

AVATAR ADI DA SAMRAJ: In every moment you must turn the situation of your life into Ruchira Avatara Bhakti Yoga by exercising devotion to Me. There is no moment in any day wherein this is not your Calling. This is what you must do. You must make every moment into this Yoga by using the body, emotion, breath, and attention in self-surrendering devotional Contemplation of Me. All of those four principal faculties must be turned to Me. By constantly turning to Me, you "yoke" yourself to Me, and that practice of linking (or binding, or connecting) to Real God is religion. Religion, or Yoga, is the practice of moving out of the egoic (or separative, or self-contracted) disposition and state into Oneness with That Which is One, Whole, Absolute, All-Inclusive, and Beyond. [December 2, 1993]

As everyone quickly discovers, it is only possible to practice Ruchira Avatara Bhakti Yoga moment to moment when you establish a foundation of supportive self-discipline that enables you to reel in your attention, energy, and feeling from their random wandering. And so Ruchira Avatar Adi Da has Given unique and extraordinarily full Instruction on a complete range of functional, practical, relational, and cultural disciplines for His first-congregation and second-congregation devotees. These disciplines are not methods for attaining Happiness, but are the present-time expression of prior Happiness:

AVATAR ADI DA SAMRAJ: I do not require the discipline of conventional renunciation. Nor do I allow commitment to the karmas of self-indulgence. My devotees serve Me through the humorous discipline of an ordinary pleasurable life. This is the foundation of their practice of the Way of Adidam.

The "ordinary pleasurable life" of which Avatar Adi Da Samraj Speaks is not based on any kind of attempt to achieve immunity from the inevitable wounds of life. Rather, it is based on the always present disposition of True Happiness—the disposition of ego-transcendence through self-surrendering, self-forgetting Contemplation of Ruchira Avatar Adi Da in every moment. Therefore, the "ordinary pleasurable life" of Avatar Adi Da's devotees involves many practices that support and develop the simplicity and clarity of Happiness and self-transcendence. These practices are "ordinary" in the sense that they are not Enlightenment in and of themselves, but they are, rather, the grounds for a simple, mature, pleasurable, and truly human life, devoted to Real-God-Realization.

These practices in the Way of Adidam include cultural disciplines such as morning and evening meditation, devotional chanting and sacramental worship, study-"consideration" of Ruchira Avatar Adi Da's Wisdom-Teaching, formal weekly retreat days, extended weekend retreats every two to three months, an annual meditation retreat of ten days to six weeks. The life of practice also includes the adaptation to a pure and purifying diet, free from toxifying accessories (such as tobacco, alcohol, caffeine, sugar, and processed foods) and animal products (such as meat, dairy products, and eggs).

Meditation is a unique and precious event in the daily life of Avatar Adi Da Samraj's devotees. It offers the opportunity to relinquish outward, body-based attention and to be alone with Adi Da Samraj, allowing yourself to enter more and more into the sphere of His Divine Transmission.

The practice of sacramental worship, or "puja", in the Way of Adidam is the bodily active counter - part to meditation. It is a form of ecstatic worship of Avatar Adi Da Samraj, using a photographic representation of Him and involving devotional chanting and recitations from His Wisdom-Teaching.

You must deal with My Wisdom-Teaching in some form every single day, because a new form of the ego's game appears every single day. You must continually return to My Wisdom-Teaching, confront My Wisdom-Teaching.
Avatar Adi Da Samraj

The beginner in Spiritual life must prepare the body-mind by mastering the physical, vital dimension of life before he or she can be ready for truly Spiritual practice. Service is devotion in action, a form of Divine Communion.

Avatar Adi Da Samraj Offers practical disciplines to His devotees in the areas of work and money, diet, exercise, and sexuality. These disciplines are based on His own human experience and an immense process of "consideration" that He engaged face to face with His devotees for more than twenty-five years.

There is also a discipline of daily exercise which includes morning calisthenics and evening Hatha Yoga exercises. There is progressive adaptation to a regenerative discipline of sexuality and sexual energy. And, as a practical foundation for your personal life and the life of the community of practitioners, there is the requirement to maintain yourself in full employment or full-time service, in order to support the obligations of the sacred institution (the Eleutherian Pan-Communion of Adidam) and the cooperative community organization (the Ruchirasala of Adidam).

All of these functional, practical, relational, and cultural disciplines are means whereby your body-mind becomes capable of effectively conducting Ruchira Avatar Adi Da's constant Blessing-Transmission. Therefore, Ruchira Avatar Adi Da has made it clear that, in order to Realize Him with true profundity—and, in particular, to Realize Him most perfectly, to the degree of Divine Enlightenment—it is necessary to be a formally acknowledged member of either the first or the second congregation engaging the total practice of the Way of Adidam.

One of the ways in which Ruchira Avatar Adi Da Communicates His Divine Blessing-Transmission is through sacred places. During the course of His Teaching and Revelation Work, He Empowered three Sanctuaries as His Blessing-Seats. In each of these Sanctuaries—the Mountain Of Attention in northern California, Love-Ananda Mahal in Hawaii, and Adidam Samrajashram in Fiji—Ruchira Avatar Adi Da has Established Himself Spiritually in perpetuity. He has lived and Worked with devotees in all of His Sanctuaries, and has created in each one special holy sites and temples. In particular, Adidam Samrajashram—His Great Island-Hermitage and world-Blessing Seat—is Ruchira Avatar Adi Da's principal Place of Spiritual Work and Transmission, and will remain so forever after His physical Lifetime. Formally acknowledged devotees are invited to go on special retreats at all three Sanctuaries.

The Mountain Of Attention Sanctuary of Adidam

Love-Ananda Mahal

**Adidam Samrajashram
(Naitauba, Fiji)**

Ruchira Avatar Adi Da writes in *Eleutherios (The Only Truth That Sets The Heart Free)*:

I Have Come to Found (and, altogether, to Make Possible) a New (and Truly "Bright") Age of mankind, an Age That will not begin on the basis of the seeking mummery of ego-bondage, but an Age in Which mankind will apply itself, apart from all dilemma and all seeking, to the Inherently Harmonious Event of Real existence (in the Always Already present-time "Bright" Divine Reality That Is the One and Only Reality Itself).

In the brief period of two and a half decades, and in the midst of this "dark" and Godless era, Ruchira Avatar Adi Da has established His unique Spiritual culture. He has created the foundation for an unbroken tradition of Divine Self-Realization arising within a devotional gathering aligned to His fully Enlightened Wisdom, and always receiving and magnifying His Eternal Heart-Transmission. Nothing of the kind has ever existed before.

There are great choices to be made in life, choices that call on the greatest exercise of one's real intelligence and heart-impulse. Every one of us makes critical decisions that determine the course of the rest of our lives—and even our future beyond death.

The moment of discovering the Divine Avatar, Adi Da Samraj, is the greatest of all possible opportunities. It is pure Grace. How can an ordinary life truly compare to a life of living relationship and heart-intimacy with the greatest God-Man Who has ever appeared—the Divine in Person?

Call or write one of our regional centers and sign up for "The Only Truth That Sets the Heart Free", our preliminary course that prepares you to become a fully practicing devotee of Avatar Adi Da Samraj. Or sign up for any of our other classes, correspondence courses, seminars, events, or retreats. Or call to order more books and continue your reading.

Respond now. Do not miss this miraculous opportunity to enter into direct relationship with Real God.

The Eleutherian Pan-Communion of Adidam

AMERICAS
12040 North Seigler Road
Middletown, CA 95461
(800) 524-4941
(707) 928-4936

PACIFIC-ASIA
12 Seibel Road
Henderson
Auckland 1008
New Zealand
64-9-838-9114

AUSTRALIA
P.O. Box 460
Roseville, NSW 2069
Australia
61-2-9416-7951

EUROPE-AFRICA
Annendaalderweg 10
6105 AT Maria Hoop
The Netherlands
31 (0)20 468 1442

THE UNITED KINGDOM
London, England
0181-7317550

FIJI
P.O. Box 4744
Samabula, Suva, Fiji
381-466

E-MAIL: correspondence@adidam.org

We also have centers in the following places. For their phone numbers and addresses, please contact one of the centers listed above or visit our website: **http://www.adidam.org**.

Americas
San Rafael, CA
Los Angeles, CA
Seattle, WA
Denver, CO
Chicago, IL
Framingham, MA (Boston)
Potomac, MD
    (Washington, DC)
Kauai, HI
Quebec, Canada
Vancouver, Canada

Pacific-Asia
Western Australia
Melbourne, Australia

Europe-Africa
Amsterdam, The Netherlands
Berlin, Germany

The Sacred Literature of Ruchira Avatar Adi Da Samraj

Start by reading *The Promised God-Man Is Here*, the astounding story of Avatar Adi Da's Divine Life and Work.

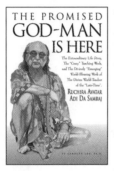

The Promised God-Man Is Here

The Extraordinary Life-Story, The "Crazy" Teaching-Work, and The Divinely "Emerging" World-Blessing Work Of The Divine World-Teacher Of The "Late-Time", Ruchira Avatar Adi Da Samraj, by Carolyn Lee, Ph.D.—the profound, heart-rending, humorous, miraculous, wild—and true—story of the Divine Person Alive in human Form. Essential reading as background for the study of Avatar Adi Da's books.

See My Brightness Face to Face

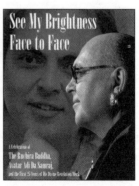

A Celebration of the Ruchira Avatar, Adi Da Samraj, and the First Twenty-Five Years of His Divine Revelation Work—a magnificent year-by-year pictorial celebration of Ruchira Avatar Adi Da's Divine Work with His devotees, from 1972 to 1997. Includes a wealth of selections from His Talks and Writings, numerous Stories of His Divine Work told by His devotees, and over 100 color photographs.

$19.95, 8"x10" quality paperback, 200 pages

THE FIVE BOOKS OF THE HEART
OF THE ADIDAM REVELATION

Aftter reading *The Promised God-Man Is Here*, continue reading *The Five Books Of The Heart Of The Adidam Revelation*. In these five books, Avatar Adi Da Samraj has distilled the very essence of His Eternal Message to every one, in all times and places.

BOOK ONE:
Aham Da Asmi
(Beloved, I Am Da)

The "Late-Time" Avataric Revelation Of The True and Spiritual Divine Person (The egoless Personal Presence Of Reality and Truth, Which Is The Only Real God)

The most extraordinary statement ever made in human history. Avatar Adi Da Samraj fully Reveals Himself as the Living Divine Person and Proclaims His Infinite and Undying Love for all and All.

$7.95, 4"x7" paperback, 222 pages

BOOK TWO:
Ruchira Avatara Gita
(The Way Of The Divine Heart-Master)

The "Late-Time" Avataric Revelation Of The Great Secret Of The Divinely Self-Revealed Way That Most Perfectly Realizes The True and Spiritual Divine Person (The egoless Personal Presence Of Reality and Truth, Which Is The Only Real God)

Avatar Adi Da Offers to every one the ecstatic practice of devotional relationship to Him—explaining how devotion to a living human Adept-Realizer has always been the source of true religion, and distinguishing true Guru-devotion from cultism.

$7.95, 4"x7" paperback, 254 pages

BOOK THREE:

Da Love-Ananda Gita
(The Free Gift Of The Divine Love-Bliss)

*The "Late-Time" Avataric Revelation Of The Great
Means To Worship and To Realize The True and
Spiritual Divine Person (The egoless Personal Presence
Of Reality and Truth, Which Is The Only Real God)*
Avatar Adi Da Reveals the secret simplicity at the
heart of Adidam—relinquishing your preoccupation
with yourself (and all your problems and your suffering) and,
instead, Contemplating Him, the "Bright" Divine Person of Infinite
Love-Bliss.

$7.95, 4"x7" paperback, 234 pages

BOOK FOUR:

Hridaya Rosary
(Four Thorns Of Heart-Instruction)

*The "Late-Time" Avataric Revelation Of The Universally
Tangible Divine Spiritual Body, Which Is The Supreme
Agent Of The Great Means To Worship and To Realize
The True and Spiritual Divine Person (The egoless
Personal Presence Of Reality and Truth, Which Is
The Only Real God)*
The ultimate Mysteries of Spiritual life, never before revealed. In
breathtakingly beautiful poetry, Avatar Adi Da Samraj sings of the
"melting" of the ego in His "Rose Garden of the Heart".

$7.95, 4"x7" paperback, 358 pages

BOOK FIVE:

Eleutherios
(The Only Truth That Sets The Heart Free)

*The "Late-Time" Avataric Revelation Of The "Perfect
Practice" Of The Great Means To Worship and To
Realize The True and Spiritual Divine Person (The
egoless Personal Presence Of Reality and Truth,
Which Is The Only Real God)*
An address to the great human questions about
God, Truth, Reality, Happiness, and Freedom. Avatar Adi Da Samraj
Reveals how Absolute Divine Freedom is Realized, and makes an
impassioned Call to everyone to create a world of true human free-
dom on Earth.

$7.95, 4"x7" paperback, 270 pages

THE SEVENTEEN COMPANIONS
OF THE TRUE DAWN HORSE

Once you have read *The Five Books Of The Heart Of The Adidam Revelation*, you are ready to continue with *The Seventeen Companions Of The True Dawn Horse*. These seventeen books are "Companions" to *The Dawn Horse Testament*, Avatar Adi Da's great summary of the Way of Adidam (p. 211). Here you will find Avatar Adi Da's Wisdom-Instruction on particular aspects of the true Spiritual Way, and His two tellings of His own Life-Story, as autobiography (*The Knee Of Listening*) and as archetypal parable (*The Mummery*). Avatar Adi Da created the Canon of His Sacred Literature in late 1997 and early 1998, and the Dawn Horse Press is currently in the process of publishing the "Seventeen Companions" and *The Dawn Horse Testament*.

BOOK ONE:

<u>Real</u> God <u>Is</u> The Indivisible Oneness Of Unbroken Light

Reality, Truth, and The "Non-Creator" God
In The True World-Religion Of Adidam

The Nature of Real God and of the cosmos. Why ultimate questions cannot be answered either by conventional religion or by science.

BOOK TWO:

The Truly Human New World-Culture Of <u>Unbroken</u> Real-God-Man

The <u>Eastern</u> Versus The <u>Western</u> Traditional Cultures
Of Mankind, and The Unique New <u>Non-Dual</u> Culture
Of The True World-Religion Of Adidam

The Eastern and Western approaches to religion, and life altogether—and how the Way of Adidam goes beyond this apparent dichotomy.

BOOK THREE:

The <u>Only</u> Complete Way To Realize The Unbroken Light Of <u>Real</u> God

An Introductory Overview Of The "Radical" Divine Way
Of The True World-Religion Of Adidam

The entire course of the Way of Adidam—the unique principles underlying Adidam, and the unique culmination of Adidam in Divine Enlightenment.

BOOK FOUR:

The Knee Of Listening

The Early-Life Ordeal and The "Radical"
Spiritual Realization Of The Ruchira Avatar

Avatar Adi Da's autobiographical account of the years from His
Birth to His Divine Re-Awakening in 1970. Includes a new chapter,
"My Realization of the Great Onlyness of Me, and My Great Regard
for My Adept-Links to the Great Tradition of Mankind".

BOOK FIVE:

The Method Of The Ruchira Avatar

The Divine Way Of Adidam Is An ego-Transcending
Relationship, Not An ego-Centric Technique

Avatar Adi Da's earliest Talks to His devotees, on the fundamental
principles of the devotional relationship to Him and "radical"
understanding of the ego. Accompanied by His summary statement
on His relationship to Swami Muktananda and on His own unique
Teaching and Blessing Work.

BOOK SIX:

The Mummery

A Parable About Finding The Way To My House

A work of astonishing poetry and deeply evocative archetypes. The
story of Raymond Darling's growth to manhood and his search to
be reunited with his beloved, Quandra.

BOOK SEVEN:

He-and-She Is Me

The Indivisibility Of Consciousness and Light
in The Divine Body Of The Ruchira Avatar

One of Avatar Adi Da's most esoteric Revelations—His Primary
"Incarnation" in the Cosmic domain as the "He" of Primal Divine
Sound-Vibration, the "She" of Primal Divine Light, and the "Son" of
"He" and "She" in the "Me" of His Divine Spiritual Body.

BOOK EIGHT:

Divine Spiritual Baptism
Versus Cosmic Spiritual Baptism

Divine Hridaya-Shakti Versus Cosmic Kundalini Shakti
In The Divine Way Of Adidam

The Divine Heart-Power (Hridaya-Shakti) uniquely Transmitted by
Avatar Adi Da Samraj, and how it differs from the various traditional
forms of Spiritual Baptism, particularly Kundalini Yoga.

THE DAWN HORSE TESTAMENT

The Dawn Horse Press

In addition to Avatar Adi Da's 23 "Source-Texts", the Dawn Horse Press offers hundreds of other publications and items for meditation and sacred worship—courses, videotapes, audiotapes, compact discs, magazines, photos, incense, sacred art and jewelry, and more. Call today for a full catalog of products or visit our website (http://dhp.adidam.org) where you will find full-color images of all our products and on-line ordering.

For more information or a free catalog:
CALL TOLL-FREE 1-800-524-4941
(Outside North America call 707-928-4936)
Visit us on-line at **http://dhp.adidam.org**
Or e-mail: **dhp@adidam.org**
Or write:
THE DAWN HORSE PRESS
12040 North Seigler Road
Middletown, CA 95461 USA

We accept Visa, MasterCard, personal checks, and money orders. In the USA, please add $4.00 (shipping and handling) for the first book and $1.00 for each additional book. California residents add 7.25% sales tax. Outside the USA, please add $7.00 (shipping and handling) for the first book and $3.00 for each additional book. Checks and money orders should be made payable to the Dawn Horse Press.

An Invitation to Support Adidam

Avatar Adi Da Samraj's sole Purpose is to act as a Source of continuous Divine Grace for everyone, everywhere. In that spirit, He is a Free Renunciate and He owns nothing. Those who have made gestures in support of Avatar Adi Da's Work have found that their generosity is returned in many Blessings that are full of His healing, transforming, and Liberating Grace—and those Blessings flow not only directly to them as the beneficiaries of His Work, but to many others, even all others. At the same time, all tangible gifts of support help secure and nurture Avatar Adi Da's Work in necessary and practical ways, again similarly benefiting the entire world. Because all this is so, supporting His Work is the most auspicious form of financial giving, and we happily extend to you an invitation to serve Adidam through your financial support.

You may make a financial contribution in support of the Work of Adi Da Samraj at any time. You may also, if you choose, request that your contribution be used for one or more specific purposes.

If you are moved to help support and develop Adidam Samrajashram (Naitauba), Avatar Adi Da's Great Island-Hermitage and World-Blessing Seat in Fiji, and the circumstance provided there and elsewhere for Avatar Adi Da and the other members of the Ruchira Sannyasin Order, the senior renunciate order of Adidam, you may do so by making your contribution to The Love-Ananda Samrajya, the Australian charitable trust which has central responsibility for these Sacred Treasures of Adidam.

To do this: (1) if you do not pay taxes in the United States, make your check payable directly to "The Love-Ananda Samrajya Pty Ltd" (which serves as the trustee of the Foundation) and mail it to The Love-Ananda Samrajya at P.O. Box 4744, Samabula, Suva, Fiji; and (2) if you do pay taxes in the United States and you would like your contribution to be tax-deductible under U.S. laws, make your check payable to "The

214

Eleutherian Pan-Communion of Adidam", indicate on your check or accompanying letter that you would like your contribution used for the work of The Love-Ananda Samrajya, and mail your check to the Advocacy Department of Adidam at 12040 North Seigler Road, Middletown, California 95461, USA.

If you are moved to help support and provide for one of the other purposes of Adidam, such as publishing the sacred Literature of Avatar Adi Da, or supporting either of the other two Sanctuaries He has Empowered, or maintaining the Sacred Archives that preserve His recorded Talks and Writings, or publishing audio and video recordings of Avatar Adi Da, you may do so by making your contribution directly to The Eleutherian Pan-Communion of Adidam, specifying the particular purposes you wish to benefit, and mailing your check to the Advocacy Department of Adidam at the above address.

If you would like more information about these and other gifting options, or if you would like assistance in describing or making a contribution, please write to the Advocacy Department of Adidam at the above address or contact the Adidam Legal Department by telephone at (707) 928-4612 or by FAX at (707) 928-4062.

Planned Giving

We also invite you to consider making a planned gift in support of the Work of Avatar Adi Da Samraj. Many have found that through planned giving they can make a far more significant gesture of support than they would otherwise be able to make. Many have also found that by making a planned gift they are able to realize substantial tax advantages.

There are numerous ways to make a planned gift, including making a gift in your Will, or in your life insurance, or in a charitable trust.

If you would like to make a gift in your Will in support of the work of The Love-Ananda Samrajya: (1) if you do not pay taxes in the United States, simply include in your Will the statement, "I give to The Love-Ananda Samrajya Pty Ltd, as trustee of The Love-Ananda Samrajya, an Australian charitable trust, P.O. Box 4744, Samabula, Suva, Fiji, _____" [inserting in the blank the amount or description of your contribution]; and (2) if you do pay taxes in the United States and you would like your contribution to be free of estate taxes and to also reduce any estate taxes payable on the remainder of your estate, simply include in your Will the statement, "I give to The Eleutherian Pan-Communion of Adidam, a California non-profit corporation, 12040 North Seigler Road, Middletown, California 95461, USA, _____" [inserting in the blank the amount or description of your contribution].

To make a gift in your life insurance, simply name as the beneficiary (or one of the beneficiaries) of your life insurance policy the organization of your choice (The Love-Ananda Samrajya or The Eleutherian Pan-Communion of Adidam), according to the foregoing descriptions and addresses. If you are a United States taxpayer, you may receive significant tax benefits if you make a contribution to The Eleutherian Pan-Communion of Adidam through your life insurance.

We also invite you to consider establishing or participating in a charitable trust for the benefit of Adidam. If you are a United States taxpayer, you may find that such a trust will provide you with immediate tax savings and assured income for life, while at the same time enabling you to provide for your family, for your other heirs, and for the Work of Avatar Adi Da as well.

The Advocacy and Legal Departments of Adidam will be happy to provide you with further information about these and other planned gifting options, and happy to provide you or your attorney with assistance in describing or making a planned gift in support of the Work of Avatar Adi Da.

Further Notes to the Reader

An Invitation to Responsibility

Adidam, the Way of the Heart that Avatar Adi Da has Revealed, is an invitation to everyone to assume real responsibility for his or her life. As Avatar Adi Da has Said in *The Dawn Horse Testament Of The Ruchira Avatar*, "If any one Is Interested In The Realization Of The Heart, Let him or her First Submit (Formally, and By Heart) To Me, and (Thereby) Commence The Ordeal Of self-Observation, self-Understanding, and self-Transcendence." Therefore, participation in the Way of Adidam requires a real struggle with oneself, and not at all a struggle with Avatar Adi Da, or with others.

All who study the Way of Adidam or take up its practice should remember that they are responding to a Call to become responsible for themselves. They should understand that they, not Avatar Adi Da or others, are responsible for any decision they may make or action they may take in the course of their lives of study or practice. This has always been true, and it is true whatever the individual's involvement in the Way of Adidam, be it as one who studies Avatar Adi Da's Wisdom-Teaching or as a formally acknowledged member of Adidam.

Honoring and Protecting the Sacred Word through Perpetual Copyright

Since ancient times, practitioners of true religion and Spirituality have valued, above all, time spent in the Company of the Sat-Guru (or one who has, to any degree, Realized Real God, Truth, or Reality, and who, thus, Serves the awakening process in others). Such practitioners understand that the Sat-Guru literally Transmits his or her (Realized) State to every one (and every thing) with whom (or with which) he or she comes in contact. Through this Transmission, objects, environments,

217

and rightly prepared individuals with which the Sat-Guru has contact can become Empowered, or Imbued with the Sat-Guru's Transforming Power. It is by this process of Empowerment that things and beings are made truly and literally sacred, and things so sanctified thereafter function as a Source of the Sat-Guru's Blessing for all who understand how to make right and sacred use of them.

Sat-Gurus of any degree of Realization and all that they Empower are, therefore, truly Sacred Treasures, for they help draw the practitioner more quickly into the process of Realization. Cultures of true Wisdom have always understood that such Sacred Treasures are precious (and fragile) Gifts to humanity, and that they should be honored, protected, and reserved for right sacred use. Indeed, the word "sacred" means "set apart", and, thus, protected, from the secular world. Avatar Adi Da has Conformed His body-mind Most Perfectly to the Divine Self, and He is, thus, the most Potent Source of Blessing-Transmission of Real God, or Truth Itself, or Reality Itself. He has for many years Empowered (or made sacred) special places and things, and these now Serve as His Divine Agents, or as literal expressions and extensions of His Blessing-Transmission. Among these Empowered Sacred Treasures is His Wisdom-Teaching, which is Full of His Transforming Power. This Blessed and Blessing Wisdom-Teaching has Mantric Force, or the literal Power to Serve Real-God-Realization in those who are Graced to receive it.

Therefore, Avatar Adi Da's Wisdom-Teaching must be perpetually honored and protected, "set apart" from all possible interference and wrong use. The fellowship of devotees of Avatar Adi Da is committed to the perpetual preservation and right honoring of the sacred Wisdom-Teaching of the Way of Adidam. But it is also true that, in order to fully accomplish this, we must find support in the world-society in which we live and in its laws. Thus, we call for a world-society and for laws that acknowledge the Sacred, and that permanently protect It from insensitive, secular interference and wrong use of any kind. We call for, among other things, a system of law that acknowledges that the Wisdom-Teaching of the Way of Adidam, in all Its forms, is, because of Its sacred nature, protected by perpetual copyright.

We invite others who respect the Sacred to join with us in this call and in working toward its realization. And, even in the meantime, we claim that all copyrights to the Wisdom-Teaching of Avatar Adi Da and the other sacred Literature and recordings of the Way of Adidam are of perpetual duration.

We make this claim on behalf of The Love-Ananda Samrajya Pty Ltd, which, acting as trustee of The Love-Ananda Samrajya, is the holder of all such copyrights.

Avatar Adi Da and the Sacred Treasures of Adidam

True Spiritual Masters have Realized Real God (to one degree or another), and, therefore, they bring great Blessing and introduce Divine Possibility to the world. Such Adept-Realizers Accomplish universal Blessing Work that benefits everything and everyone. They also Work very specifically and intentionally with individuals who approach them as their devotees, and with those places where they reside and to which they Direct their specific Regard for the sake of perpetual Spiritual Empowerment. This was understood in traditional Spiritual cultures, and, therefore, those cultures found ways to honor Adept-Realizers by providing circumstances for them where they were free to do their Spiritual Work without obstruction or interference.

Those who value Avatar Adi Da's Realization and Service have always endeavored to appropriately honor Him in this traditional way by providing a circumstance where He is completely Free to do His Divine Work. Since 1983, He has resided principally on the island of Naitauba, Fiji, also known as Adidam Samrajashram. This island has been set aside by Avatar Adi Da's devotees worldwide as a Place for Him to do His universal Blessing Work for the sake of everyone, as well as His specific Work with those who pilgrimage to Adidam Samrajashram to receive the special Blessing of coming into His physical Company.

Avatar Adi Da is a legal renunciate. He owns nothing and He has no secular or religious institutional function. He Functions only in Freedom. He, and the other members of the Ruchira Sannyasin Order, the senior renunciate order of Adidam, are provided for by The Love-Ananda Samrajya, which also provides for Adidam Samrajashram altogether and ensures the permanent integrity of Avatar Adi Da's Wisdom-Teaching, both in its archival and in its published forms. The Love-Ananda Samrajya, which functions only in Fiji, exists exclusively to provide for these Sacred Treasures of Adidam.

Outside Fiji, the institution which has developed in response to Avatar Adi Da's Wisdom-Teaching and universal Blessing is known as "The Eleutherian Pan-Communion of Adidam". This formal organization is active worldwide in making Avatar Adi Da's Wisdom-Teaching available to all, in offering guidance to all who are moved to respond to His Offering, and in providing for the other Sacred Treasures of Adidam, including the Mountain Of Attention Sanctuary (in California) and Love-Ananda Mahal (in Hawaii). In addition to the central corporate entity known as The Eleutherian Pan-Communion of Adidam, which is based in California, there are numerous regional entities which serve congregations of Avatar Adi Da's devotees in various places throughout the world.

Practitioners of Adidam worldwide have also established numerous community organizations, through which they provide for many of their common and cooperative community needs, including those relating to housing, food, businesses, medical care, schools, and death and dying. By attending to these and all other ordinary human concerns and affairs via self-transcending cooperation and mutual effort, Avatar Adi Da's devotees constantly free their energy and attention, both personally and collectively, for practice of the Way of Adidam and for service to Avatar Adi Da Samraj, to Adidam Samrajashram, to the other Sacred Treasures of Adidam, and to The Eleutherian Pan-Communion of Adidam.

All of the organizations that have evolved in response to Avatar Adi Da Samraj and His Offering are legally separate from one another, and each has its own purpose and function. Avatar Adi Da neither directs, nor bears responsibility for, the activities of these organizations. Again, He Functions only in Freedom. These organizations represent the collective intention of practitioners of Adidam worldwide not only to provide for the Sacred Treasures of Adidam, but also to make Avatar Adi Da's Offering of the Way of Adidam universally available to all.

INDEX

NOTE TO THE READER: Page numbers in **boldface** type refer to the Scriptural Text of the *Da Love-Ananda Gita*. All other page numbers refer to the introductions, endnotes, and the back matter.

229

I do not simply recommend or turn men and women to Truth. I *Am* Truth. I Draw men and women to My Self. I *Am* the Present Real God, Desiring, Loving, and Drawing up My devotees. I have Come to Be Present with My devotees, to Reveal to them the True Nature of life in Real God, which is Love, and of mind in Real God, which is Faith. I Stand always Present in the Place and Form of Real God. I accept the qualities of all who turn to Me, dissolving those qualities in Real God, so that *Only* God becomes the Condition, Destiny, Intelligence, and Work of My devotees. I look for My devotees to acknowledge Me and turn to Me in appropriate ways, surrendering to Me perfectly, depending on Me, full of Me always, with only a face of love.

I am waiting for you. I have been waiting for you eternally.

Where are you?

AVATAR ADI DA SAMRAJ
1 9 7 1